I shall pass through this world but once. Any good therefore that I can do or any kindness that I can show to any human being, let me do it now. Let me not defer or neglect it for I shall not pass this way again.

EX LIBRIS

DEMOCRACY
and the
WORK PLACE

DEMOCRACY

AND THE

WORK PLACE

by H. B. Wilson

BLACK ROSE BOOKS — Montréal

BLACK ROSE BOOKS NO. C 15

First Edition 1974

Hardcover — ISBN: 0-919618-23-5

Paperback — ISBN: 0-919618-22-7

BLACK ROSE BOOKS LTD.
3934 rue St. Urbain
Montréal 131, Québec.

Printed and bound in Québec, Canada

I wish to express my sincere thanks to the trustees of the Boag Foundation Ltd., Vancouver, B.C. A generous grant from the Boag Foundation made possible the extensive travel and research necessary to complete this book.

I would also like to thank the many people who assisted me in my research and those who offered constructive criticism and advice.

This book is dedicated to my father who always believed that there must be a better way to organize work.

references

Footnotes distract me. I am always torn between chasing down the little numbers (which usually refer me to 'ibid' or 'op cit') or ignoring them and perhaps missing something vital.

Selective bibliographies annoy me. They are usually an unselective listing of books with no apparent purpose other than to impress the reader with the amount of reading done by the author.

If a book interests me and I want to know more about its subject without duplicating the author's research, some references are helpful. Most helpful are those that give some idea of how relevant the references are to the subject. With this in mind, I have included a number of references in the text of this book and their relevance will be apparent from their context. At the end of the book are comments on a number of books and articles. These are arranged to assist readers who wish to read more about some of the topics in this book.

contents

contents

chapter one

introduction

THIS is not a book about philosophy. It is an attempt to apply a philosophy, or set of ideals, to a particular problem — the problem of management.

The set of ideals which I have tried to apply to management may be described as socialist-humanist. Their purpose is to enable each person to develop his full human potential in harmony with his fellow men and his environment.

When our lives are fragmented our humanity is diminished. We may spend an hour in the morning for the purpose of getting to work; seven or eight hours during the day for the purpose of earning money; more time for the purpose of getting home from work; evenings for a variety of purposes; nights for the purpose of sleeping so we can repeat the process the next day. This activity presumably has both an immediate purpose and an ill-defined long range purpose — perhaps the anticipation of a three week holiday next summer, or a comfortable retirement at 65.

By fragmenting our lives into bits of activity we alienate ourselves from our fellow men and our environment. People and things become hostile objects which we must overcome. The space between home and work is alien territory occupied by alien cars and drivers impeding our objective of crossing the territory as quickly as possible.

Our working hours are dominated by alien bosses and hostile co-workers competing for the promotion that we want for ourselves for some egoistic or materialistic purposes.

In our homes we protect ourselves against all that is outside. Outside we battle the elements. We can enjoy moderate sunshine, but wind, rain and snow can be hostile elements. Our alienation from our natural environment leads to proposals for domed cities and the creation of a controlled artificial environment.

When we have won all the battles, acquired our material possessions and retired in our comfortable, secure, air-conditioned environment, we find that we don't know how to live *now*. We are unprepared for activity that has no purpose beyond itself. We cannot accept that after years of planned, purposeful activity we haven't achieved instant happiness. The realization that it was all wasted is suppressed by sudden death or by engaging in trivial activities for the purpose of filling in the time until death.

When a child responds to the question, "Why did you do it?" with, "I just did it," he is answering the question. Our failure to recognize his response as an answer indicates that we have lost the ability to 'just do things'. Our activity must have some object separate from the activity itself.

When a man sits under a tree whittling, he just sits under a tree whittling. If his whittling produces a pleasing object, then the object is pleasing, but it is not the purpose of his activity. The activity itself is satisfying.

Few of us can spend our lives just whittling. Now and for the foreseeable future we must spend a significant part of our waking hours working. If during that time we can be engaged in a satisfying activity just working, we will have gone some way towards learning to develop our potential to live now. A fundamental change in the way work is organized in enterprises is not the full answer to alienation but it is a precondition to living in harmony with our environment, our fellow men and ourselves.

chapter two

prerequisites

AGREEMENT on the desirability of the objectives outlined in the introduction is far from universal but it is much more widespread than might be expected. There are, it is true, men like the executive vice-president of one of Canada's largest corporations who said in a private discussion, "I consider the employees as one element in the production process, no more and no less important than any other element".

An examination of working conditions in most industries might suggest that the values implicit in his statement are those prevalent amongst managers. There are, however, many managers who feel strongly that the work done by their employees should be satisfying. The fact that there is a difference between their stated belief and their practice is not necessarily an indication of hypocrisy. It may indicate a lack of understanding of the conditions necessary to make work satisfying. Other explanations include yielding to pressure from above or a lack of confidence in their ability to put their beliefs into practice. Often these two factors go hand-in-hand.

Managers in both publicly and privately-owned enterprises are responsible for producing measurable results — measurable in dollars or number of units. They are accountable for past performance — not for future quality of life. They are accountable for artificially delineated activities considered to be within the proprietorship of the enterprise. Social costs of alcoholism, crime and family breakups, caused by alienating work conditions, are outside the area of accountability and therefore not the responsibility of managers.

Only very determined and very confident managers are willing to risk extending their areas of accountability and responsibility beyond the prescribed boundaries.

Much the same difficulty applies to socialists — most of whom would agree with the objectives in the introduction. Socialist parties have usually gained power in times of severe economic problems. Regardless of their desire for change in the quality of life, they have faced immediate quantitative problems — reduce unemployment, increase production, redistribute income, provide housing, etc. Faced with the immediate problems and often also the need to account to the electorate a few years hence, socialist governments seldom have had the confidence to apply their professed ideals to the solution of the qualitative problems.

Again, this is more an indication of lack of confidence than of hypocrisy. Perhaps now, more than at any other time, there are more socialists and humanists who agree that it is essential to make fundamental changes so that work can be a satisfying, liberating experience. They are supported by many more people who may not have articulated a coherent philosophy but who know instinctively that there is something wrong with the meaningless 'rat race' which typifies most work in industrialized societies.

There is, therefore, very significant support for the objectives. What we lack is agreement that the objectives can be reached and that we should start now with our attempts to reach them.

It is easy to dismiss an idea with the statement, "It's fine, but we have to be practical." To be practical we place people in rows along assembly lines, we place people in rows at desks, we place people in rows at cash registers. We ask them to remain passively turning the right bolts or pushing the right keys as the work comes to them. Each week we pay them an agreed wage until, in desperation to prove their humanity and restore their dignity, they go on strike. To be practical we agree to pay a higher wage.

We must keep the economy growing when the workers return to their respective slots in rows of houses or rows of apartments. To be practical we must convert the workers into consumers of things produced by other rows of people.

The logic of being practical has led us to cover some of our best agricultural land with pavement and concrete, to convert our lakes into cesspools, to destroy our wilderness areas, to create urban sprawls so we can escape the air pollution of urban centres. It is the logic of Alice in Wonderland. Each act by itself is logical but the whole is devoid of reason.

We do have to be practical but being practical means acting not on the basis of isolated bits of logic, but on the basis of reason. It hardly seems reasonable to drift in a direction which leads to the destruction of humanity.

It has often been suggested that the direction of social movement can be changed without changing working conditions. In support of this is the assumption that work is a necessary evil to be endured in order to provide the financial resources to create a full life outside working hours. This assumption leads to the conclusion that we should concentrate on training for leisure and on the improvement in the quality of leisure-time activities.

The assumption and conclusion are fallacious. Work is a very significant factor in the lives of adults and usually the elimination of the need to work does not eliminate the desire to work. There are various psychological explanations for this, but regardless of the explanation, the fact of the importance of work remains. Its importance precludes the possibility of most people passively accepting orders from an authoritarian hierarchy during working hours and then becoming full participants in life, after working hours. The passive role is reinforced too strongly while involved in the important work activity.

Of course the direction of social movement can be changed by governments which exercise authoritarian control over leisure in the same way employers exercise control over work. That 'solution' is self-defeating for those who are concerned about the development of human potential.

The possibility of most work, as we now know it, being eliminated by automation is sometimes put forward as an argument against the need to find ways of making work more satisfying. The argument is based on a misconception of the potential of computers. As the role of computers is discussed in some detail later in this book, it is sufficient at this stage to mention that we are nowhere near being able to replace manpower with computer power on a massive scale. Even if it were economically feasible, it wouldn't work because there are fundamental differences between the abilities of computers and humans.

Our technology is sufficiently advanced for us to meet our material needs with shorter working hours if our resources were used efficiently. This leads to the possibility of ignoring work alienation on the grounds that work will occupy a small part of our lives.

This conclusion assumes that those who are born in countries that have abundant natural resources and advanced technology, have no obligation towards people born in other countries. Such a view is, for socialist-humanists, morally indefensible.

Agreement that work *should* be a satisfying non-alienating experience is more widespread than agreement than it *can* be. It can only be so when authoritarian management is eliminated. This inevitably leads to replacement by some form of industrial democracy. The concept of industrial democracy is not new but very little has been written to illustrate how we can move from where we are, to its attainment.

Canada is not on the verge of a people's revolution. With some exceptions, workers are not going to rise and take control of our factories, offices and governments. The political left and the trade union movement must act as catalysts in a process which can bring about fundamental change.

I am not suggesting that spontaneous action towards industrial democracy cannot take place. It can and it does particularly in Québec where a form of industrial democracy was a key issue in the strikes at Firestone and Canadian Gypsum. Community reaction and eventual take-over of the shut-down pulp and paper mill in Timiscaming provides another example of industrial democracy emerging spontaneously.

There is considerable interest in industrial democracy within the Letter Carriers' Union of Canada with which I am now associated. In August 1973, a wild-cat strike by its Ottawa Local succeeded in removing an undesirable boss. It didn't succeed in winning the right of the workers to decide who should be appointed to management positions but it showed that it could decide who should not be appointed. This created greater awareness among the workers of their potential to control their work environment.

The trade union establishment contains people who identify their own interests with the interests of the capitalists. Higher profits are good because they enable higher wage demands and, so long as working conditions are tolerable, that represents the limit of their interests. The mass media tends to create the impression that this is the prevalent attitude amongst union leaders. My own impression, based on association with numerous active trade-unionists over a good many years, is that the conservative element represents a minority. There is another minority group of social democrats scarred by the battles against communist infiltration in the late 1940's and early 50's. The largest group within Canadian unions, however, comprises men and women who desire a basic change in our social and economic relationships, brought about through constitutional means.

In January 1972, the C.L.C. held a two-day conference in Ottawa to discuss industrial democracy. The conference was closed to the press but according to a C.L.C. news release, "This conference is not a policy-making conference but its outcome may serve as a guide for a policy statement to be submitted to the C.L.C. biennial convention in May, 1972." Papers delivered by Donald MacDonald, Joe Morris (respectively President and Vice-President of the C.L.C.) and other prominent trade unionists, were distributed to the press.

A consistent theme occurs throughout the papers. Stripped of its rousing rhetoric it goes like this:

Managers are necessary.
The interests of management and labour conflict.
Unions must represent the interest of labour.
If unionists participate in management through workers' councils, or as members of management boards, they cannot at the same time represent labour's interests.
Therefore, participation in management is bad.
But industrial democracy is good.
Therefore, industrial democracy must be defined as an extension of collective bargaining to reduce management's residual rights. To simplify this process, we should have a social democrat government.

It did occur to some of the speakers that workers might imagine they were capable of managing their own lives at work and at play. Donald MacDonald dismissed this by saying, "In another time and in another place this solution to social and economic problems went by the name of the dictatorship of the proletariat."

Gordon McCaffrey of the C.L.C. put it this way, in a background paper prepared for the conference, ". . . it is impossible to transfer the concept of 'one man, one vote' to industry without at the same time destroying the basis of private ownership. Investors would be reluctant, if not foolhardy, to risk their capital in an enterprise in which workers had a right to participate in decision-making on an equal basis."

The dangers of token participation in management were stressed by several speakers and they are well known to trade unionists in most industrialized capitalist countries. Token participation enables manipulation by management and reduces labour's strength in collective bargaining and therefore runs counter to trade union interests.

The historical role of unions has been as parties in an adversary system. Union representatives bargain with capital representatives in an effort to get a bigger slice of the pie. On the broader front, unions have worked for a more humane society through political action and many humanitarian causes have been promoted by unions. With the numerous activities of Canadian unions, collective bargaining remains as their most important activity and for a few unions carrying on in the Sam Gompers tradition, almost the only activity.

Bitter experience with the combined power of governments and capital has caused many workers in Québec to question the traditional role of unions. The Québec government's refusal to bargain in the spring of 1972 with the common front of public service employees, and the subsequent jailing of the leaders of the front, was one more illustration of the fact that gains made by collective bargaining are limited to the maximum that capitalists and their governments decide to grant. Of course, the same is true in most provinces but it has been demonstrated more frequently and more dramatically in Québec than in most other provinces. The realization of this has led to demands for workers' control of Québec industries — demands phrased in the rhetoric of the Left.

In English speaking Canada, we may be more influenced by other historical events which remind us that dictatorships of the left and right emasculated the powers and independence of unions and converted them into organizations serving the aims of the state.

But advocates of industrial democracy do not ask unions to sacrifice their organizations to an abstract ideal. They ask unionists to take the next step towards the goal that has always been theirs — the preservation of the dignity of man. Along the way, the immediate battlefield will change as it has done in the past. The unions have scored victories in the battles for abolition of child labour, for the eight hour day, for recognition, for an end to racial and sexual discrimination, for some restrictions on arbitrary actions by bosses. Next must come the battle for an end to a corporate system that sets one man over another — that is, an end to the boss-employee relationship. Such a step does not signal the advent of dictatorship but the extension of democracy.

There is a danger, however, in thinking that industrial democracy can be achieved by transplanting the structures of political or parliamentary democracy into corporations. Parliamentary democracy is based on the election of representatives to various levels of government and allowing those representatives to decide what is best for us. If, after four or five years, we think that they have made the wrong decisions, we supposedly can replace them with other representatives. But it will not work in corporations.

A system of worker representation on the governing boards of corporations presupposes the need for a distinction between those who decide what is to be done and those who do it. It preserves a we-they split and thereby preserves one of the major causes of worker alienation. No doubt worker representation in corporate governing boards reduces the chance of inhumane actions by the corporate decision-makers but, as the German system of co-management demonstrates, it makes little difference in the daily work life of the men on the shop floor or the girls at typewriters. The real change comes from *direct* participation in and control over the work environment and the way work is done.

But we must start where we are with corporations having hierarchical management organizations with ultimate power at the top. During the transition to industrial democracy, workers, through their local unions, will require representation on boards that control corporations. Here we run into the objection that representation on management boards would conflict with the unions' responsibility to represent the workers' interests against management.

The objection is valid only if it is assumed that traditional organizations are retained and that representation in those organizations is a final objective. But the real objective is direct participation by workers and indirect representation is just a temporary expedient. It is against the objective of direct participation and control, that the unions must examine their roles.

If we accept the elitist view that there must always be the managers and the managed, then unions must not compromise their position as representatives of the managed by sharing the jobs of the managers. If, however, we accept the view that people have differing talents but that the possession of a particular talent should not give a few people power over many people, then there is no need for indefinite continuation of the adversary system.

Industrial democracy, which ends the management-labour adversary system, does not end the importance of unions. On the contrary, union experience with cooperative and democratic organizations and unionists concern with the dignity of labour, are vital to the success of industrial democracy. Too often unionists have to run all-out to avoid losing ground. The battles are often not for better wages but enough to keep up to the increase in the cost of living; not for more job security but to prevent more insecurity; not for better working conditions but to prevent worse conditions. These battles must be carried on so long as the structures that make them necessary exist. Marginal gains will be made from time to time but the important victory will be won only by changes in corporate relationships.

Many Canadians passively accept authoritarian structure and decisions in the belief that "they" know what's best for us. One of the most dramatic illustrations of this was the strong support for the Federal Government when it invoked the War Measures Act in October 1970, and the drop in support for the N.D.P. which alone opposed the Act.

Several psychologists and sociologists have attempted to measure and explain variations in the tendency of people to accept authoritarianism. Whatever the reasons for accepting authoritarianism, it is a factor which must be considered in working towards industrial democracy. Industrial democracy implies self-management in place of authoritarian management, but the grass roots demand for self-management is not now strong enough to lead to its widespread realization. A catalyst is required.

My hope is to outline a practical plan for experimenting with industrial democracy. The experiment could be conducted within crown corporations or agencies under provincial social democratic governments. Much of what follows deals with the initial steps which are necessary to reach the final objectives. It is impossible to describe, in detail, the structures and organizations which would ultimately emerge because in a truly democratic society, organizations will be shaped by those participating in them. It would be presumptuous to predict the outcome, but as a matter of conviction, I prefer the unknown results of democracy to the predetermined results of autocracy.

This does not imply that everything has to be left to chance. On the contrary, positive action must be taken to break down authoritarian management structures so they can be replaced by a system of management that will lead to demands for greater participation by employees and finally lead to demands for self-management. The preliminary structures must have built-in safeguards so that power shifts towards employees as rapidly as their demands and alternative structures enable the shift.

No matter how many safeguards are built into the preliminary structure, the shift from top-down to bottom-up democracy could be delayed by people in key positions. They must be committed to industrial democracy and not to token participation. This effectively excludes most people who have spent years studying management in universities, unless they left behind most of what they learned about management when they left university.

Most of the writing on industrial democracy focuses on its relevance to workers in factories, mines and others who are described as blue collar workers. This is to be expected as it is there that the hardships are most obvious. The men working in mines, factories and construction sites are those most exposed to heat and cold, injuries and accidental deaths. They are the first to be laid off when business is slack and they are the last to receive benefits when business is good. But let us not overlook the plight of the so-called white collar workers who, in Canada, now outnumber the blue collars. Not only have the terms blue collar and white collar lost their literal meanings, their figurative meanings have also been lost.

There are some white collar jobs left where workers can take pride in their work, just as there are some left in the factories. But there aren't many. Most of the office clerks, sales clerks and clerks in the various service industries perform tasks that are as repetitious and meaningless as the tasks performed by workers on assembly lines. Even that insidious status symbol of a monthly salary, rather than an hourly wage, has largely disappeared. Many clerks attempt to enhance their status by speaking contemptuously of manual workers, just as many manual workers speak contemptuously of the clerks. But the fundamental problem of alienation is the same for all workers and no proposal for industrial democracy will succeed unless it applies to all workers.

Before we experiment we usually want to feel that there is a reasonable chance of success. Just before the plunge, idealism tends to give way to pragmatism. We wonder, "Will it work?"

I believe it will.

Summary

For the forseeable future, work will continue to play a dominant role in our lives. To overcome the alienation caused by present forms of work organization, workers must take control of their own working environment. This can happen spontaneously in some enterprises or it can be speeded up by the influence of progressive trade unionists and by legislation introduced by socialist governments. This requires a re-examination of conventional wisdom and a willingness to break with tradition.

chapter three

power and authority

WHAT we may do at work or play is circumscribed by laws, regulations, rules and customs. Even the anarchist movements of the first half of this century and the New Left movements of the 1960's found that group activity required members of the group to follow rules in the form of establishing customs.

Rules or laws are not necessarily causes of alienation but they may be symptoms of a membership which is alienated from the group structure. This applies whether the group consists of citizens of a country, the players on an amateur hockey team, the employees of a corporation or the members of a trade union. When the members of the group refer to 'they', the members are alienated from the formal structure of the group. When 'they' make unacceptable rules or laws, those rules or laws are symptoms of alienation.

How we react to rules or laws that affect us, depends on whether or not we feel that the people who make the rules have a right to do so. We react differently to what we consider to be power and what we consider to be authority. The distinction is a subjective one, varying from person to person and from one period in history to another. Nevertheless, it is possible to make some generalized statements about power and authority which are useful in developing a non-alienating corporate structure.

If I point a gun at your head and demand $10, you will recognize that I am, at least temporarily, exercising power. Unless you are exceptionally well qualified in self-defense, you will follow my orders at the time and attempt to retaliate later by the use of police power. Our relationship is a hostile one, as I have, in your opinion, no *right* to take your money.

If we work together and I have been asked by other workers to take up a collection for a fellow employee who has had a serious accident, and I ask you to contribute $10, you will recognize my right to make the request. You do so because I have been authorized to make the request by other workers. So long as the amount is reasonable and you can afford it, you will respond favourably. Our relationship is not hostile. You recognize that my authority is legitimate because I have derived my authority from our peers. The difference between that and the power I derived from the gun, is obvious.

A third example will illustrate a more subjective element in the distinction between power and authority.

Assume that I am your boss and you recognize that I have some rights or authority over your work. I say to you, "Our company has accepted a quota of $5,000 for the X Charitable Fund. To meet that quota, we need $10 from each employee in this department. Would you prefer to contribute by cash or by payroll deduction?"

You will probably feel that this is a non-legitimate use of power, one step removed from the gun episode. Others might feel that it is a legitimate use of my authority as a boss because they interpret authority as something derived from above or Above.

As the creator or author of all things, God has been the only source of authority. Kings and popes derived their authority directly from God and delegated part of it to princes and priests. Only a few cynics thought it strange that God should consistently transfer his authority to the victor of the most recent battle or revolt. Thus, power and authority were always hand-in-hand.

The Pope and a few secular leaders still claim to rule by divine authority. In most monarchies, including Canada, certain formalities of divine authority remain, but these are generally recognized as formalities. Nevertheless, the idea of authority derived from above is deeply ingrained in most of us and enables us to accept the boss's right to issue orders. Our boss has derived his authority from his boss, who derived it from his boss and so on up to the owners of the corporation. And how does ownership give them authority?

The authority of corporation owners is derived from law but the law only makes legitimate the power that they hold. If we can no longer see ourselves as part of a divine chain of command, which integrates power and authority as it runs down the corporate hierarchy, we can no longer be part of the whole. We are, instead, subject to the dictates of a hostile "they".

The long struggle for political democracy has been a struggle against the exercise of power and for the exercise of authority delegated by the people. The current struggle for industrial democracy is essentially the same. It cannot succeed unless it has a structure that replaces power derived from ownership, by authority derived from employees.

Because the distinction between power and authority is partly subjective and changes over time, it is impossible to describe an organizational structure for industrial democracy that will be valid for all time. The best we can do is outline a structure that is appropriate at the moment and is responsive to change.

A corporate organizational structure that is appropriate at the moment is one in which authority is derived in a manner considered legitimate by the employees. This means something less than full workers' control as that is not generally accepted as the legitimate source of authority by people with no previous experience in shaping their own work environment. A structure responsive to change is one in which the current legitimate authority cannot be converted into permanent power. It must respond to demands for full workers' control because those demands will increase once a start is made. Lack of response will lead to the tokenism of current participative management techniques and the continuation of alienation in employment. This can be illustrated by what happens in many families.

Young children accept the fact that their parents have legitimate authority over them. They may object to some of the rules made by their parents but they do not question their right to make the rules.

As a child grows older and asks, "Why should I do that?" he is no longer prepared to accept the answer, "Because I say so." He may know that he has to do it because his parents say so, but that doesn't make it right. In adolescence, the 'Because I say so' response is unacceptable unless the child believes that his parents act with divine authority. Failing that he realizes that they are simply exercising power — some of it sanctioned by law and some of it economic blackmail.

When parents convert temporary authority over infants to power over adolescents, they can expect their child's alienation to be expressed in the form of rebellion. The analogy with corporate power and authority breaks down if carried too far, but it does help illustrate the need to respond to change arising from increased understanding.

In his book *Political Parties,* Robert Michels sums up his iron law of oligarchy with the words, "It is organization which gives birth to the domination of the elected over the electors, of the mandatories over the mandators, of the delegates over the delegators. Who says organization says oligarchy."

If his law is valid, temporary authority will always be converted into permanent power. Although Michels cites numerous examples in support of his law, his conclusion may have been determined more by his elitist tendencies than by scholarly research. His pessimistic conclusions can safely be rejected, but we cannot deny that there is a strong tendency to convert legitimate authority into personal power. If we wish to maintain an organizational structure that is responsive to change and to the will of the members, it is necessary to build in safeguards.

Most trade unions and democratic socialist parties have constitutions that appear to ensure that all major decisions will be authorized by the members or by elected representatives who are accountable to the members. Elected representatives must seek re-election at regular intervals if they wish to continue in office.

In addition to these almost standard constitutional provisions, there are a number of widely used safeguards against abuse of authority. These include limits on the number of times a person may be re-elected to the same position and provisions for challenges, appeals and special membership meetings. The safeguards are not entirely successful, and officers are sometimes able to retain their positions even after they have lost the support of the members. Information is the key to converting authority into power — or more accurately, the opportunity to withhold information is the key.

Dictatorships are invariably secretive and their ability to retain power is often related to their ability to control information. The power of the FBI in the United States and the R.C.M.P. in Canada is directly related to their own secret information. Both organizations can prevent people from obtaining employment on the strength of secret information in secret files — information that is impossible to challenge because it is unknown to the victim. These are examples of the use of arbitrary power within democratic countries, justified by successive governments on the grounds of 'national security'. They are saying, in effect, that the control of information by dictatorships is bad but its control by democracies is good because it benefits the nation. As the imposition of the War Measures Act illustrated, it is difficult to remain just a little bit pregnant with power.

When attending meetings or conventions where decisions are made, most of us hope that our own views will prevail. Elected officials of democratic organizations are no different. When an elected official enters a contentious debate with, "Fellow delegates, if you were aware of all of the information considered by your officers in formulating this resolution, you would not hesitate to support it," he is using, perhaps legitimately, a very persuasive argument.

It is a short step from this to consciously withholding information to strengthen his influence. When information is withheld for that purpose, his influence becomes power. Although he and his fellow officers may believe they are acting in the best interest of the members, they will destroy true democratic participation by the members. Even if control over information is not exercised to increase power, the belief in the need for secrecy indicates an elitist attitude. How else could elected officers believe that they are more capable than the members, to assess information?

In most capitalist countries, secrecy is a way of life so deeply ingrained that few leaders even think about it. If industrial democracy is to be viable, a deliberate effort must be made to provide employees with access to all relevant information.

Throughout this book I have recommended a number of organizational changes to aid in the transition to industrial democracy. Nowhere have I given a blueprint of the ideal organization because there can be no permanently ideal organization. The most that can be done is to describe certain of its characteristics such as:

(1) Enables maximum participation
(2) Legitimate authority cannot be converted into power
(3) Responsive to change

Maximum participation is not finite. As workers gain experience and confidence in managing their own activities, the range of participation can increase. As participation increases, the concept of legitimate authority changes and the organizational structure must respond to this change. If it does not, authority becomes power and a 'we-they' conflict develops.

The cycle in which participation increases the ability to participate and the ability to participate changes the concept of authority, is self-perpetuating, provided structural changes are rapid enough to allow increasing participation. There is no point at which we can say "stop!, we have reached the ideal". That, in effect, is what an organization blueprint would say and if the blueprint could be created in advance, the democratic process would be unnecessary.

When we predetermine the formal structure of an organization, we expect people to fit the structure. Initially the fit may be satisfactory, but attitudes change through participation in the organization and the initial structure becomes less satisfactory. The changes brought about by participation in a democratic process at work and the concomitant elimination of boss-employee relationships, make it impossible to determine the best formal structures for industrial democracy beyond the early stages.

In most corporations, the workers are subjected to a variety of often conflicting pressures from several sources. First, the demands of the job to be done put pressure on the employees. Additional pressures come from foremen, supervisors, managers, technical experts, control techniques and endless petty rules and regulations. An employee is the man in the middle, as illustrated by the diagram below.

Foremen and supervisors
Job demands
Managers
Rules and regulations

Employee
Control techniques
Technical Experts

The pyramid structure of management arose from the assumption that soldiers needed to be controlled by their superior officers so that they would follow orders when told to risk their lives killing unknown strangers for unknown reasons. Technical problems require most corporations to use technical experts to supplement the management pyramid. These experts are given power to exert additional pressures on the employees. It is a tribute to the ingenuity of employees that they are able to be as productive as they are while subjected to so many external pressures.

This shift from coercive power to legitimate authority, brought about by industrial democracy, will remove the pressure from employees and focus attention on the job to be done. This is illustrated by the diagram below.

Employees
Technical Experts
The Job
Coordinators
Controls

Hierarchical or pyramid organizations devote a large part of their efforts to controlling people. The approach suggested above enables the resources of an organization to be devoted to the job and is therefore more efficient. But attempts to use it to increase efficiency will fail because such attempts would be just another form of manipulation. Success depends upon using it only because of respect for human dignity. The difference is not just one of semantics. Respect for human dignity is fundamental to the success of industrial democracy, for industrial democracy is not just another way of getting work done. It is a way of living and developing during the work day.

Summary

In enterprises, managers have power to control workers and their work environment. The process leading towards industrial democracy aims at replacing management power with authority derived from the workers.

Safeguards are required to prevent people from blocking the transition to industrial democracy by trying to retain power. One of the important safeguards is to end secrecy in decision-making.

ERRATA

PAGES 27 and 28 — Diagrams omitted are as below:

a)   From coercive power

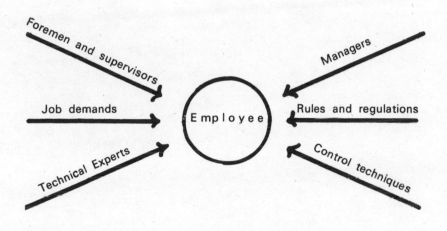

b)   To legitimate authority

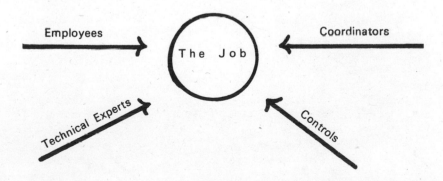

chapter four

trade-offs

MUCH of my preliminary research for this book was directed towards finding a way to reconcile our desire for efficient production of the material goods we require and our desire to organize production so as to provide job satisfaction and reduce alienation. It seemed to me that at some point it was necessary to trade off the spiritual against the material. Obviously, there are many unpleasant jobs which must be done and many unpleasant, but apparently efficient methods of doing other jobs. Foremost among these methods are the assembly lines.

My research led to an examination of the trade-off point in other countries where the question of reconciling material and spiritual values might be expected to arise. My impression, based on a fair bit of direct observation, is that the Soviet Union tends to trade off in favour of production. Sweden has taken a non-dogmatic approach to getting the best of both worlds, but the trend now is towards job satisfaction. Americans, and to a lesser extent, Canadians, are wedded to the virtues of efficiency but all bright young managers have learned that participation improves job satisfaction and leads to greater efficiency. Autocratic management is out and participative management is in —

or at least enough token participation to manipulate employees into thinking they are part of the team.

There have been numerous experiments which clearly demonstrate the economic benefits of participation. Paul Blumberg's book, *Industrial Democracy: The Sociology of Participation,* (Constable, London 1968) provides an exceptionally good review of a number of these experiments.

As my research advanced, I realized I was working on a nonproblem. No trade-off between material and spiritual values is necessary or possible.

I concluded that all direct cost reductions achieved through alienation or other things which tend to reduce human fulfillment are lost through indirect costs. This loss is in economic terms, not just in human values. It follows that we should reject the idea of sacrificing human values for increased production.

This conclusion may seem idealistic and only applicable to a highly industrialized society where routine tasks can be automated but that argument overlooks the fact that tasks cannot be classified as satisfying or non-satisfying. Such classifications assume that a task has meaning apart from the person who performs it. Both empirical evidence and philosophical reasoning indicate that the two cannot be separated.

Two main factors determine the extent to which a task will alienate — personal characteristics and external circumstances. Because of our personal characteristics, many people would find working as a dentist very unpleasant. Even though the tasks performed by dentists are very important and useful, they are only satisfying to people with a particular combination of personal characteristics.

Each person must determine for himself — often through trial and error — what tasks are satisfying to his personal characteristics. It does not follow that many people are happy on assembly lines or performing a routine clerical task year after year. Some people in such jobs may resist change but that can usually be explained by the fact that they are seeking security through the knowledge that everything will be all right during their working hours.

While seeking security in that way is understandable, it is almost certain to lead to an extension of the same techniques to leisure hours. That inevitably leads to narrowing horizons and undeveloped human potential.

To avoid alienation, the individual must feel that he is performing a task suitable to his personal characteristics and that the task is significant in the sense that it contributes to something worthwhile.

External factors can greatly change an individual's idea of the kind of work which is significant. During the siege of Leningrad, removing corpses and many other normally grim jobs were more significant than pleasant tasks. Following popular revolutions, people willingly subject themselves to long hours of hard work on tasks which at other times would be alienating. In wars, individualists willingly submit to rigid discipline so long as they believe that their greatest contribution can be made that way. In the 1950's the 'Organization Man' existed because it was possible to sustain faith in corporations as saviours. Now only banks seem to be able to do some of that with their employees.

Note that as external factors change, so do the individual ideas of satisfaction change, but governments, corporations and other organizations are always too slow in reacting to the change and alienation spreads. Tasks which were meaningful, or appeared meaningful, became meaningless. Alienation leads to dissatisfaction and loss in production.

As only the individual can determine what is satisfying for him, it is impossible to create an ideal organization, define the jobs, then find people to fill them. No matter what testing techniques are used, it won't take long before many of the people are dissatisfied with their work.

When the objectives of an organization are clear, the people directly concerned with meeting those objectives are the ones best able to determine how to do it.

This approach to organizing seems to have a flaw because some jobs might not get done. However, if a job *needs* to be done and is not done, the need will become apparent. The apparent need for the job to be done, automatically creates the external conditions necesssary to make the job satisfying. With some exceptions, an individual with the personal characteristics which make that job satisfying will recognize the need and fill it.

Some jobs are, by any reasonable standards, unpleasant and undesirable. They include jobs that are dull, repetitious and meaningless, jobs that demand excessive physical exertion and jobs that subject the workers to temperature extremes, foul odours and health hazards. It is no coincidence that such jobs are generally among the lowest paid jobs in Canada. They are filled by people whose only alternative is unemployment, and the low wage costs offer no incentive to employers to seek alternative ways of doing the jobs.

Workers managing their own affairs could do much immediately to eliminate or relieve unpleasant jobs. Intensive government-sponsored technological research could supplement the process. Job rotation or sharing of unpleasant tasks can give further relief when elimination is not possible.

Let us assume that a ship with 400 passengers is cracked up on a reef near a remote Pacific island. In keeping with tradition the captain goes down with his ship but the 400 passengers, a random collection of men, women and children, all survive and reach the island. The climate is moderate, ample fruit grows on the island and fresh water is plentiful. There is no immediate threat of death through exposure or starvation but also no immediate promise of comfort or a varied diet.

Let us assume also that the passengers are somehow aware that at least several months will pass before they are rescued. Now let us consider the forms of organization that are likely to develop.

It will soon become apparent that variation in the diet is desirable and fishing would likely be the quickest way to provide variety. Someone with experience in fishing and perhaps some knowledge of how to make lines, hooks or nets will emerge as a natural leader of the fishing group. Others who have some interest or aptitude for fishing will follow the natural leader.

Someone else with experience in carpentry or construction will become the natural leader of a group concerned with shelters. Somone else, perhaps with experience as a chef or housewife, will become the leader of a group organizing meals so that the fish and fruit can be prepared and distributed in an equitable manner. Some necessary, but unpleasant jobs may lack volunteers and will be rotated and shared by all.

Over a period of time, other groups will develop around natural leaders in order to provide more comforts and entertainment. If the people remain stranded for a long period of time, some of the early leaders will be replaced simply because others are recognized as more appropriate. This will occur without formalities, but in order to preserve their leadership positions, some leaders may suggest that a formal procedure be followed for replacing them. At this stage, a certain amount of resentment will occur and some people will feel that they are being coerced by the leaders. If there is no formal method of selecting the leaders or if the formal method is democratic, cooperation can be expected and resentment will be minimal.

Now let us go back to the same set of assumptions with one important change. Let us assume that the ship's captain survived and maintained his authority on the island.

Being a well-trained bureaucrat, he will endeavour to shortcut the natural process of selecting leaders and immediately establish what seems to him to be an efficient organization. He will recognize the need to have a group of people catching fish, another group collecting fruit and another erecting shelters. Being aware that the most efficient bureaucracy operates with specialized labour and clear-cut lines of authority and responsibility, he will go about selecting people to manage the groups. He will weigh up the qualifications of those claiming expertise in fishing, construction and so on, and select the best qualified to manage the groups. In return for managing the groups, they will be awarded extra rations.

Women, children and old people will be assigned menial tasks and of course receive correspondingly smaller rations. As would be expected, since the captain assumes all of this responsibility, he is entitled to the largest share of the rations.

It does not take much imagination to realize that the captain's organization is going to be less effective than the organization that emerged naturally. Resentment will be widespread. Struggles will develop for the privileged positions and people will be assigned to tasks in which they have little or no interest.

The analogy between these two situations and industrial democracy and autocratic management may seem to be a little far-fetched. It is, however, a useful analogy, as what happens in almost all formal organizations is that they begin with a theory of organization and then fit the people into the positions required by theory. Industrial democracy, on the other hand, begins with people and their needs and then allows the organization to develop naturally.

In a democratic enterprise, the workers not only make decisions as a group, they accept responsibility for their decisions. There are times, however, when decisions must be made by specific individuals and responsibility accepted by specific individuals. Authoritarians usually believe that most decisions must be made by individuals to avoid inefficiency and compromise. Presumably, they imagine themselves best qualified for that role. Socialists usually believe in the merits of democratic decision making, but within their own ranks they will often bypass it with the explanation, "We must be businesslike." It is worthwhile exploring the point at which individual decisions should give way to democratic decisions, or democratic decisions should give way to individual decisions.

First, a few remarks on being businesslike. As an employee, auditor, systems analyst, tax assessor and consultant, I have worked with dozens of businesses. My experience indicates that being businesslike implies being inefficient. Being businesslike implies wasting resources by petty power struggles, the destruction of human dignity through stupid autocratic decisions, acceptance of bad ideas because they come from the right source and rejection of good ideas because they come from the wrong source, blatantly ignoring facts because they contradict accepted theories. The only place I have seen that could outdo a typical business in these attributes is the Department of National Defence. No democratically controlled organization would tolerate the inefficiency of autocratic business management.

Still, the myth of business efficiency persists, so let us turn from a subjective to an objective examination of the evidence.

Profit is the measure of success in private enterprise. It is the reward for efficiency which, we are told, ultimately benefits everyone in Canada. Figures showing total profits in Canada in a particular year are of no use in judging success because profit is calculated in many different ways and we have nothing to compare the total with. We can, however, do a simple extrapolation. If private enterprise were successful by its own criterion, the profits would be high enough to permit substantial reinvestment and this would be reflected in a high rate of economic growth. But our growth rate does not compare favourably with the more advanced socialist and social democratic countries, even though we supplement investment funds generated through profits, by foreign investment.

Perhaps profits and economic growth are not the sole criterion of success. We are told that one of the virtues of private enterprise is that it encourages risk-taking which opens up our country and develops our resources. This myth conveniently ignores the fact that the financial risks involved in opening Canada with canals, railways, highways, air-lines and pipelines, were almost all assumed by governments and not by private enterprise. Exploration and development of our natural resources follow the same pattern. Not only do our mining companies pay very low taxes, we subsidize their exploration, extraction and transportation to refineries. When the federal government in 1970 and 1971 proposed a slight increase in taxes and decrease in subsidies, private enterprise made it abundantly clear that it was unwilling to assume any of the risks of exploiting our natural resources.

Mining companies may be extreme in their unwillingness to take risks, but they are not unique. Almost every new plant built anywhere in Canada in the past decade was built with subsidies — often with sub-sidies from all three levels of government. Companies building in poorer areas can expect to be subsidized and to have any risk under-written by either the federal or provincial government. So much for risk-taking in private enterprise.

Perhaps the strength of private enterprise lies in its ability to efficiently provide the public with goods and services. Certainly our stores offer a variety of luxury goods to affluent customers, but what about necessities?

The tremendous gap between food prices paid by consumers and prices received by farmers tells us something about the efficiency of the food processing and distribution industries. The inability of private enterprise to provide adequate housing has led to several forms of government intervention. In Ontario, the Tory government enjoys closer ties with the insurance industry than are seemly even for a Tory govern-ment. Despite these ties, the Tories were forced to conclude that government run hospital and medical insurance is more efficient than their friends could offer. Experience in Manitoba and Saskatchewan indicates that the same is true of automobile insurance.

If private enterprise were successful in meeting our needs for goods and services, we would not have about 20% of our population living in poverty, nor would we have such extreme regional disparity, high unemployment and economic booms and busts.

All right, so private enterprise is not perfect and it isn't efficient on all fronts. But what about innovation, creativity, imagination, research, new ideas — all those things that are stifled by bureaucracies and flourish in private enterprise where individual initiative is free to lead us on to bigger and better things. Yes, what about that? It is precisely on that front that private enterprise chalks up its greatest failure.

Large and medium size businesses in Canada have adapted products to improve their efficiency or make them more marketable. So far as I can tell, they have not developed a single new product or conception for at least the past 20 years. If there has been an exception, I haven't been able to find it. There have been new developments and concepts as a result of scientific research in Canada but these have taken place in government agencies, universities and occasionally in small independent operations. Some innovative adaptations of new concepts have taken place in smaller businesses. Big business has concentrated on marketing adaptations even though it receives government subsidies for research. The failure in this area is so significant that it merits further analysis.

Our capitalist system has at times been referred to as an entrepreneurial system. The reference had some slight justification 100 years ago, but none now, even though a few entrepreneurs survive in the system.

An entrepreneur is a person who has an idea for a new product or service. He implements his idea by assembling and directing the appropriate manpower and equipment. If successful, he profits from its implementation, and imitators, rather than innovators, will follow his lead.

A frequent argument in support of capitalism is that it encourages entrepreneurial development by offering high financial rewards to innovators. The argument is based on a misunderstanding of both the capitalist system and the entrepreneurs.

Profit is not the motive for innovation. Men such as da Vinci, Franklin, Bell, Nobel and the Wright brothers didn't sit down one day and say: "I'm going to think up an idea for a new product so I can get rich." Nobel, in particular, did get very rich from his idea for dynamite but he didn't get his idea from the possibility of getting rich. The distinction is important because this incorrect cause and effect relationship is basic to capitalism. Capitalists infer that because some innovators get rich, therefore the chance to get rich causes innovation. This is as logical as inferring that it rains because people put on raincoats. There is a connection, of course, but the raincoats don't cause the rain, nor does the chance for wealth cause the innovative idea.

What a political-economic system can do is either encourage or discourage the implemention of innovation ideas. In modern capitalism large corporations are the dominant force and they discourage innovation. This is widely recognized by managers and in management literature and much effort has been devoted to solving the problem. But it can't be solved in corporations with hierarchical organizations.

The basic characteristic of an innovative idea is that it jumps beyond the next step that can be calculated by anyone with the required technical knowledge. To illustrate, cars can be improved by applying technical knowledge. To find a substitute for cars that offer their convenience without their social cost requires innovation — that is, a breakthrough, or break-away from traditional thinking. Many people have the ability to be innovative, for it is a childlike quality, but as we grow older we learn to disguise it to avoid being thought of as crackpots. When we join a large corporation we get rid of it entirely or risk losing our jobs.

The only way new concepts originating at the bottom of the corporate ladder (where most people are) can get accepted at the top of the ladder is to put those concepts in writing. The written proposal must be brief (they are busy, important men near the top) and it must be logical. To be logical, it must be a next step on from what is already known and accepted. In other words, it must be a technical step and not an innovation leap. An innovative leap does not lend itself to explanation in a two page written report to faceless beings in executive suites. Imagine Al. Graham Bell, as a junior employee of a large corporation, sending a memo up the corporate ladder: "I've got a great idea for stringing wires all over the country; just hook a gadget to the wires in every house and office, run electricity through the wires, then everybody can talk to everybody else — no matter where they are." Or Nobel writing: "I can make the biggest damn bang you ever heard." Or Orville Wright saying: "Give my brother and me a few thousand dollars and a few years and we will make a machine that is heavier than air yet will carry you through the air."

"Brainstorming" was a popular fad in several corporations during the early 1960's. The idea of brainstorming was to break through traditional thought barriers by unstructured discussion with the participants tossing out ideas without premeditation. The rationale is similar to placing a monkey at a typewriter hoping that he will eventually produce a masterpiece, although in brainstorming sessions the monkeys were managers — the possessors of all corporate wisdom.

The time-honoured suggestion box and accompanying rewards for suggestions accepted, has never lived up to its expectations. Employees soon learn that suggestions are accepted only if they do not break with the corporate traditions.

Traditional autocratic management deliberately discouraged innovation by employees. Contemporary autocratic management attempts to manipulate employees towards controlled innovation (obviously a contradiction of terms). Industrial democracy opens up the possibility for innovation to all employees and creates a free environment which encourages innovative thought. This is important to both human and economic development.

When our inherent creative and innovative talents are suppressed by ourselves or by others, we are unable to achieve the satisfaction that derives from the development of our full human potential. Industrial democracy will not assure that development but it will eliminate the major obstacle placed in its way by autocratic management.

Economic development is greatly inhibited by the assumption that only a small elite in each corporation is capable of deciding the best way of doing things. Contemporary management theories recognize that people outside the managerial elite have some ideas to contribute but there is always the assumption that the elite must make the final decision. This effectively excludes the potential contribution of the great majority of working people.

Industrial democracy released that potential — not for the sake of economic development but in the name of humanity. The economic advantages that flow from the release are an added bonus.

Let us pause for a moment. I anticipate a lingering doubt in the minds of my readers. Even though my earliest recollections are of the 1930's depression and I have never had faith in the possibility of private enterprise developing an equitable society, and although as a youth I was reasonably familiar with socialist rhetoric, it took a long time for me to relate my first-hand observations to the theories I accepted. I tended to rationalize the inefficiencies of each company I worked with as resulting from the particular people in management positions. It has taken many years and experience with many companies for me to recognize that inefficiency in private business is not something explained by a unique combination of managers in each business, but is something inherent in the system itself. It has taken even longer, together with experience with a number of federal and provincial government departments and agencies, to realize that when they adopt business management techniques, they become equally inefficient. The common factor is an autocratic structure coupled with a bow in the direction of humanity. Get rid of the bow and replace it with coercion and we might (just might) get efficient production, at a high cost to humanity. Couple autocracy with a pretense of concern for humanity and you get what we have now — the worst of both worlds.

There are some fundamental differences in the attitudes of socialists and conservatives which help to explain the inefficiency of bureaucratic private enterprise.

We all seek security in our lives. Conservatives seek security by building barriers. Socialists seek security by destroying barriers. This is evident in international affairs when conservative governments seek national security by excluding supposedly hostile countries from international organizations while socialist governments attempt to include them. During the cold-war years, socialists were as much concerned as conservatives about the risk of Russian aggression but socialists believed that the risk could be reduced by reducing the barriers between Canada and the Soviet Union. Conservatives believed that the risk could be reduced by strengthening the barriers with radar lines, Bomarcs and nuclear bombs.

Within Canada, conservatives seek security from the F.L.Q. by martial law, from strikers by court injunctions, from criminals by stronger police action. Socialists seek security by eliminating the conditions which lead to violence. But it is not just in their attitudes to physical violence that the socialists and conservatives differ. Any action which reduces barriers between groups of people is a threat to the conservative mind.

Action to equalize incomes leads to the threat of having people of another class as neighbours. Free access to higher education leads to the threat of rich children having to compete with poor children. All universal schemes such as old-age pensions, medicare, family allowances and even government auto insurance, reduce barriers between groups and therefore threaten the security of the small group with which the conservative identifies.

We do not usually distinguish between the political left and right by their attitudes towards security, but the distinction is useful to understanding the difference between operating an enterprise according to conservative or socialist values.

The justification for hierarchical organization with a clear chain of command, departments with clearly defined responsibilities and individual employees with clearly defined duties, is not efficiency, but security. To work efficiently in such an organization you must find ways to break down the barriers between levels, departments and people. Only when you develop a network of personal contacts can you overcome some of the inefficiencies inherent in formal bureaucratic organization. But such an organization is necessary for the security of conservative managers who feel protected by the barriers between departments and levels. They rationalize those barriers on the grounds of efficiency even while they know they must be overcome to be efficient.

I must not go on endlessly. The evidence, subjective and objective, is there for anyone who cares to examine it without predetermining that being efficient and being businesslike are synonymous. Let us open our minds to new possibilities. In the words of Erich Fromm, "Since we do not know much about the efficiency or inefficiency of untried approaches, one must be careful in pleading for things as they are on the grounds of efficiency." (The Revolution of Hope, Bantam 1968).

Someone must be able to speak for the enterprise to outsiders. I will identify that person as a general chairman, which is more precise than director or general manager. Chairman connotes coordination, legitimate authority and accountability to the members — all essential to industrial democracy. Similarly, the various work units within an enterprise will require chairmen or coordinators selected by and accountable to the unit workers. The general chairman and the unit chairmen must have authority to make unilateral decisions when circumstances demand, but it is essential that they be accountable to the employees they represent.

Responsibility for finances presents a special problem. Until the day comes when we are all free of material temptations, people handling money and other easily disposable assets must be subject to some controls. These controls are usually an integral part of an accounting system and most professional accountants can recommend appropriate controls for different enterprises. Without going into detail of the workings of financial control systems, it should be noted that they are not just techniques for protecting an enterprise from unscrupulous employees. They also protect employees from unfounded charges of dishonesty.

Although controls need not be restrictive, the fact remains that accounting departments differ considerably from other departments or work units. The accounting department can be organized like other departments with a unit chairman accountable to the members of the department. But the accounting chairman has a much broader area of concern because he becomes, in effect, the trustee responsible for the assets of the enterprise. As trustee, he must have some authority throughout the enterprise to prevent misuse or misallocation of assets. He must be able to temporarily veto proposed expenditures by referring them back to the originators with an explanation of his reasons for referring back. As the accounting chairman or his representative should be involved in the preliminary discussions leading to a proposal for a major expenditure, differences of opinion or judgment should have been sorted then. The temporary veto power should only be exercised when there is a conflict between a specific proposal and overall policy, or when the proposal is incompatible with the financial position of the enterprise.

Except for routine decisions made by unit chairmen, decisions they must make unilaterally through time pressures, and the special authority of accounting chairmen, all major decisions can be made democratically by the people affected by the decisions. This may seem cumbersome and, quite obviously, if we consider any one specific decision that must be made, a unilateral decision-making process is more efficient. But when we consider a whole series of unilateral decisions that determine the working conditions and course of an enterprise, we are back to being businesslike. I trust that I have demonstrated that that is less efficient than being democratic. To a large extent, this is a negative defense of my conclusion that no trade-off of spiritual against material values is required. The positive case is put forward throughout the rest of this book.

Summary

Industrial democracy does not sacrifice efficiency to obtain participation. It is, in fact, more efficient than autocratic organizations. The rigid lines between departments and levels of management in business create a feeling of security for conservative minds but cause inefficiency.

Hierarchical organization inhibits innovation and ignores the talents of the majority of employees. Attempts to tap those talents while retaining the hierarchical organization are bound to fail. Artificial barriers must be eliminated in order to release the workers' potential.

chapter five

are managers necessary?

MOST discussion of industrial democracy is based on the assumption that a managerial hierarchy must exist. Unions that have opposed any form of participative management, or industrial democracy, have usually done so on the grounds that their independence would be compromised unless they maintained a clear distinction between the functions of management and labour.

But are managers necessary for enterprises to function effectively? We can approach the answer through another question, "What do managers do?" Surprisingly, almost all of the hundreds of books and thousands of articles on management avoid this question. Rosemary Steward, in her book *Managers and Their Jobs,* attempted to answer it by having 160 managers keep detailed records of how they spent their working hours over a period of four weeks. Assuming her survey was valid, the book tells us that paper work and discussions were the major time consumers, but it tells us little about what managers do as managers.

Most introductory management texts avoid the question by describing management as a universal process. The words differ slightly from book to book, but the management process is usually said to consist of:

(1) *Planning* — establishing objectives for the firm
(2) *Organizing* — deciding on the various positions to be held in the firm, the duties of each, and the relationships between each position
(3) *Staffing* — recruiting and training personnel for each position
(4) *Directing* — giving orders to, and motivating subordinates
(5) *Controlling* — checking by means of budgets, reports and visits that orders are being carried out and objectives met

More advanced management texts usually concentrate on techniques related to one or more aspects of the management process. If we seek an answer to the question, "What do managers do?" in the texts, we can conclude that they plan, organize, staff, direct and control. Although few managers can identify their daily tasks with these labels, they are useful in determining if managers are necessary.

Planning, or establishing the objectives of an enterprise is usually the prerogative of senior managers and boards of directors. In a socialist society, that must change. National and provincial economic planning, which is necessary to the development of a socialist society, must take precedence over planning within enterprises. The relationship is discussed in more detail elsewhere in this book. At present, it is enough to say that the jealously guarded right of capitalist managers to set corporate objectives must give way to social objectives established democratically.

Managers organize corporations. Then they reorganize them and keep on reorganizing them. They organize by product, then by region, then by function. They centralize, then decentralize then recentralize. They may even try centralized decentralization. A few managers get lost in each shuffle but more emerge to assure an ever expanding hierarchy. None of the reorganizations achieves the objective of creating a smoothrunning efficient corporation. Each is accompanied by a new organization chart and a manual delineating responsibilities of the departments. Therein lies the key to failure.

Organization charts and procedures manuals create walls to keep me out of your empire and you out of mine. We can work as an effective team within the enterprise only when we break down the walls and develop an informal relationship which allows us to get on with the job. As more and more informal working relationships are established, the power of control at the top is weakened and another reorganization is called for.

Effective organizations cannot be created by experts drawing on organizational theory. An effective organization exists when it has just enough formal structure to assure necessary continuity and accountability without inhibiting the development of informal relationships flexible enough to respond to change. Organization, the second step in the management process, should not, therefore, be the prerogative of managers but should result from the felt need of the workers.

Having set objectives and prepared an organizational blueprint to meet those objectives, managers staff the organization. Someone must take the initiative in this when establishing a new enterprise, but once in operation, hiring should be the responsibility of the group with which the new employee will be associated. With industrial democracy, the employees themselves accept responsibility for their work and it would be unreasonable for them to do so without control over hiring — and incidentally, discipline and firing.

The fourth step in the management process, directing, implies giving orders to subordinates. In this connection, there are interesting results of many surveys conducted to determine the attitude of factory and office workers towards their bosses. Bad bosses are ones who are constantly giving orders and interfering with the workers' jobs. Good bosses are typically described as, "He helps me if there is a problem, but otherwise he lets me get on with the job without interfering." The significant point is that the workers feel that they can get more work done when assistance replaces direction. Empirical evidence substantiates this belief.

Controlling, the final step in the management process, refers to checking results against objectives. As indicated earlier, in a socialist society, establishing objectives cannot be the prerogative of corporate managers but must be part of the democratic structures. It follows that controlling must become a form of accountability back through the democratic structures.

This analysis of the management process indicates that a hierarchy of corporate managers is unnecessary when industrial democracy is practiced in a socialist society. But the analysis is incomplete because it pays little attention to problems of coordination.

Office and plant space must be coordinated with personnel, equipment and machinery. Coordination of materials, machinery and manpower is necessary to produce goods. Production must be coordinated with storage and distribution. And so on and on. Coordination is usually done by managers and it is an essential function. But it does not have to be a management function.

Coordination is mainly a technical problem once objectives are established. There is no need for the technical problem to be handled by a manager who is a manager in the sense of being a boss.

The traditional family firms were headed by a man who was owner, manager and boss. He was able to coordinate operations by virtue of his knowledge of the operations. He was able to impose his system of coordination because he had the power to do so.

In large corporations now, department managers appear to replace the owner-bosses but the appearance is misleading. Even if each department manager were able to coordinate the activities within his department, other layers of managers higher up must coordinate the departments. In practice, many department managers lack the technical expertise required for coordination so they work with coordination plans, or schedules, produced by technicians — particularly computer personnel. They retain the traditional management-boss concept only in the sense that they retain some power to impose schedules on their subordinates. The relationship is just an indication of our authoritarian approach to corporate operations and contributes nothing to efficiency — except, perhaps, in a negative sense. When we break with the authoritarian tradition it becomes unnecessary to equate the need for coordination with the need for boss-managers.

For people to work together effectively, leadership is required and it is sometimes argued that managers are necessary to provide leadership. This argument is based on a misconception, perpetuated in management literature that distinguishes between formal and informal leadership. Formal leadership is leadership derived from holding a position of authority (e.g. management). Informal leadership is leadership recognized by a person's peers but not by the organizational structure. There is a tendency to assume that formal authority leads to formal leadership, but if this is so, the word means something different from what it means in the context of informal leadership.

Leadership is a quality we can often recognize but we find it difficult to define. It is unrelated to more obvious characteristics, as indicated by the fact that both Gandhi and Hitler had it. It is not a quality that exists in a vacuum. It manifests itself only when circumstances are right.

The life of the party who leads people in songs or games, manifests his leadership qualities in a party setting. He may, or may not, have leadership qualities that apply to work. Similarly, the leader at work may be the wallflower at a party.

Essentially, what the leader does, at work or at play, is to give direction to the group. He is unable to give direction unless he has a feeling for the mood of the group — for the type of leadership the group is unconsciously seeking. No one can exercise leadership in all circumstances and few are devoid of leadership when the circumstances are right. A man who flounders hopelessly in an urban environment might emerge as the leader of a group lost in the bush.

We can distinguish, even if we can't define, the difference between leadership and domination. Returning to a party setting, one man may quietly pluck a guitar, begin a song and find that others join in. That is leadership. Another man may loudly cajole others to join in a song and get them to do so against their wills. That is domination. The immediate results are the same, but the subjective reactions, and therefore the relationship and long term results are quite different.

Political and union conventions illustrate the difference between domination and leadership. The chairman has the job of keeping speakers on the topic and at appropriate times, closing debate so decisions can be made. Periodically, the convention gets bogged down in procedural matters and the self-styled experts in Roberts Rules of Order converge on the microphones. The moment of truth is at hand.

A chairman, if he wants to dominate the convention and has a good knowledge of the rules, can ignore the mood of the convention and bulldoze his way through the problem. He may succeed temporarily, but he will be nailed by the delegates as soon as he makes the slightest slip.

A chairman who gives leadership, relates his knowledge of the rules to the points made by the delegates, identifies the underlying problem and proposes a solution in keeping with the mood of the convention. Such a chairman helps the convention to be productive and, if he occasionally misinterprets a rule, the delegates will be tolerant.

In authoritarian enterprises, some managers happen to have leadership qualities that manifest themselves at work and they can function effectively. This, however, is a matter of chance as it is the ability to dominate, not the ability to lead, that is rewarded by promotion in authoritarian enterprises. One of the reasons for the inefficiency of most private enterprises is that we react unfavourably, and often unproductively, to domination.

If the coordinators, who will replace the supervisors, foremen and managers, are selected by the employees, there is a greater chance of getting people with appropriate leadership qualities than if they are appointed. Not every person selected will be the ideal one for the position, but the absence of perfection does not change the fact that democratic selection will lead to an overall improvement which will be reflected in increased productivity.

This point can be validated by examining the promotion process as it exists in many corporations.

A man who works hard, keeps his nose to the grindstone and causes no trouble, will usually find that virtue is its own reward. Promotion rewards go elsewhere. Specifically, they go to people who work for promotion and not for the corporation.

It is easy to overlook the fact that decisions regarding who is, or is not going to be promoted are made by people who, like all people, are influenced by the rational and irrational and the logical and emotional factors that affect decisions. They are human and therefore subject to the things that influence you and me. We tend to seek the easy way out when making decisions and so it is that the man who can easily be left behind in promotions, is left behind. He is the nose-to-the-grindstone man who can be counted on to keep his nose there. Of course he may eventually rebel or be unproductive when he realizes how the system operates, but that is a long-term problem which can be taken care of later. Meanwhile, there is the 'High profile' employee eagerly awaiting promotion.

Working up from stock-clerk to president is practical if daddy owns the company but in large corporations a more practical route is from university to management trainee, to management. It is easy to get lost in the lower levels of management. As the hierarchical pyramid rises most employees must stay at its base to support it. One rises because of outstanding technical abilities (in which case those abilities are lost to the corporation in the hope that their possessor also has administrative ability) or by keeping a 'high profile'. This is accomplished by serving on the right committees, backing the winners, taking credit for other employees' ideas and, in general, operating the system for personal advantage. Thus, the qualities that facilitate promotion are the least desirable qualities for managers.

This had been evident to me for a good many years and I was anxious to determine if it was a by-product of capitalism. Personal observation coupled with some frank discussions, indicates that the phenomenon is not unknown in the Soviet Union. The common factor in Canada and the Soviet Union is the appointment of managers by a higher level which is fed on screened, predigested information. This is bound to favour operators and manipulators rather than ability. This does not mean that people are never promoted on ability alone but it does mean that the scales are weighted the other way.

In summary, managers perform one or more of the following functions:

> Establish policy
> Coordinate operations necessary to implement policy
> Provide technical expertise to implement policy

Our economy, and to a large extent, our cultural life, is shaped by a combination of policy decisions made by managers accountable only to capitalist investors. No socialist can reconcile this with his concept of a democratic society in which the economy serves the people. In a socialist society, the basic policy decisions must result from, and be subject to, a democratic process.

Operations must be coordinated but this does not imply that they must be coordinated by a manager-boss. There is ample evidence to demonstrate that if a boss-employee relationship exists, coordination is less effective than when coordination is achieved through a democratic process. A number of examples of this are included in Paul Blumberg's "Industrial Democracy: The Sociology of Participation".

Technical expertise is required but again this does not require that technologists be bosses. In fact, their opportunity to fully utilize their expertise is lost when they assume manager-boss positions. Not only is the expertise lost; there is also a loss to humanity. Industrial democracy strives for the elimination of boss-employee relationships and this book, like all others on the subject, concentrates on the relevance of industrial democracy to employees who far outnumber bosses. But bosses, be they foremen, supervisors, managers or presidents, make up a sizeable part of our population and their future with industrial democracy should not be ignored.

When I started my first full-time office job in 1948, I was frequently given meaningless orders and often shouted at by my boss.

I vowed that if I ever became a boss, I would always explain to my staff what I was doing and why I was doing it. Since then I have spent a good many years as a boss, or manager, with power to hire, fire and give orders. I have never forgotten my vow, but I have often had to break it because the boss-employee relationship precludes complete openness and honesty. For that reason the relationship is destructive to managers, as well as employees, even though most managers seek to preserve it.

Much is made of the fact that managers assume greater responsibility than other employees and that they often must work long hours without overtime pay. This is the reason why managers are usually paid much more than non-managers and, with a capitalist value system, it is a reasonable justification. Managers take their problems home with them. Their job doesn't end at 5 o'clock. It's true but why?

One reason is that managers are captives of the myth that says that managers must work long hours. To maintain their status they must live up to the myth and take work home with them.

Another reason is that most managers lack self-confidence and therefore lack confidence in their subordinates. They are unable to delegate work. They have such difficulty doing it themselves they can't imagine it can be easily done by people below them in the hierarchy. Their own insecurity requires them to constantly check on the work done by others, so it is just as easy to do the work themselves. It is no good telling an insecure manager that he should delegate more work. He can't do it because the little faith he has in himself would be destroyed if he placed it in people below him.

The best manager I have known was the general manager of a fair size corporation and a director in several other large corporations. He seldom worked more than six hours a day because he had enough confidence and respect for himself to have confidence and respect for those who worked for him. He was exceptional as very few survive the role of boss and remain a humanist, as he did. Perhaps it was because of the accident of his birth which meant that he never had to worry about financial security. That financial security can be removed from the realm of accident and made a reality for everyone, allowing us all to concentrate on more important things.

Now back to my inability to keep my vow of openness and honesty in dealing with my staff. When a person is part way up the corporate ladder, he is privy to confidential information from above which he is not permitted to pass on to those under him. He also knows some things about members of his staff that he can't pass along to other employees. He has power to hire and fire (or at least to recommend hiring and firing, which amounts to the same thing) but he can never fully explain the basis of his action to those above or below him. Meanwhile, he is expected to run his department efficiently and accept the blame for anything that goes wrong in it. Certainly the manager living with pressures from all sides deserves some compensation or deserves to be freed from the pressure. Industrial democracy provides freedom for managers prepared to accept it.

When a man keeps other men in slavery, he himself loses his freedom. This fact, more than humanitarianism, led to the end of legalized slavery in the United States. The industrialists in the north and east of the USA realized that their desire for freedom to operate enterprises in their own interests was incompatible with a responsibility for bonded or slave labour. Ownership of slaves entailed a responsibility for the slaves even when there was no immediate use for them, whereas 'free' labourers could be hired when the need arose and dismissed when not needed. For a while, that provided a degree of freedom for managers.

Now, through laws, trade unions, social pressure and a degree of humanitarianism, managers are subject to many of the pressures of slave owners. They are no longer able to acquire and discard 'free' labour at will. They often must accept some continuing responsibility for the well-being of employees under their supervision. Only the most callous manager can ignore a continuing responsibility for the lives of people over whom he has so much control. That responsibility restricts the freedom of managers just as much as it restricts the freedom of the managed.

But managers struggle to preserve the right to restrict the freedom of others, even though they thereby restrict their own freedom. This is to be expected as we are captives of a system that equates power over others with success, just as the number of slaves owned was once a measure of success. It is not easy to learn that we cannot succeed as free human beings by restricting the freedom of others.

Nothing equals "the Boss" as a subject to be described with the richest vocabulary and greatest depth of feeling. It is true that certain personal characteristics that provoke our rage are the characteristics that help their possessors to get promoted, but it is also true that the role of boss can corrupt and bring out the worst in many people. Time and again, workers have seen a mate curse his foreman along with his fellow workers, but when promoted, he acted just like the foreman he replaced. He wasn't a hypocrite waiting for a chance to imitate the man he said he despised. He was a victim of the same pressures as the man he replaced.

If we understand why bosses behave as they do, we will not use industrial democracy to 'get the bastards'. Instead, we will recognize that they have been alienated by the system and we will attempt to help them understand the philosophy of industrial democracy. We will not always succeed. The alienation is often too great to be overcome by education and transfer out of positions of power is the only solution for those who cannot make the transition from boss to coordinator.

But we might be surprised at the number of managers who would welcome the chance to be free of the boss role but would willingly use their talents and experience as coordinators. They are the managers who have realized that self-fulfillment doesn't come through power over others but from using their talents as best they can.

Let me make it clear that I am not advocating a be-kind-to-capitalists campaign. Corporate management is frequently a function separate from corporate ownership. Even though most senior managers support the same right-wing political parties as the owners, their attitude towards the owners is often very similar to the attitude of employees towards their bosses. They feel restricted by the stupid and autocratic behaviour of the people above them. Just as many employees attribute the problem to the peculiarity of a particular boss, so do many senior managers attribute it to the peculiarities of controlling shareholders. It is that attribution which enables an employee to do back-breaking labour for eight hours a day for subsistence wages and remain a supporter of capitalism. And it is that attribution which enables senior managers to believe that they could solve the problems in the enterprise they manage if they only had more reasonable shareholders.

You can change the managers and you can change the shareholders as often as you want but nothing important will change so long as the owner-manager and boss-employee relationships remain.

Summary

The boss-employee relationship is destructive to both the boss and the employee. It is also inefficient because it diverts talents away from the objectives of the enterprise.

There is no need to have manager-bosses. With industrial democracy, the important decisions are made democratically. The important work of coordination does not have to be done by a manager-boss. It can be done more effectively by elected coordinators.

chapter six

technology and organization

W E form groups or organizations to meet our need for fellowship and to accomplish collectively what we cannot accomplish individually. The way we organize our groups is influenced by the technology at our disposal.

Primitive peoples without firearms hunted in groups which could surround and kill large animals. Cooperation and fellowship within the groups was essential. They moved with respect for and in harmony with the forest environment and their prey. Success was often accompanied by a prayer of apology for having to kill the animal.

Now any reasonably affluent 'sportsman' can buy a high-powered rifle, equip himself with everything necessary to shield him from the forest environment, then hire a guide to escort him to a place where he can pull the trigger and bag his trophy. Success is followed by the guide performing the messy operations on the dead animal — often accompanied by a silent apology.

In the sportsmans' group the members are alienated from each other by a master-servant relationship, from their environment by their protective equipment and from their prey by high-powered rifles.

When the sportsman returns to his home comforts and recounts his adventures, the hired guide is depicted as a companion and comrade; the forest environment as rugged and challenging; the kill as the culmination of complex interaction between hunter, hunted and environment. The guide's role is reduced in this final phase.

If a lie is a deliberate statement of an untruth, the sportsman's recounting is not a lie. His search for a trophy was just a small part of his reason for going hunting. More important (although unrecognized) was his search for true companionship in a natural environment unhampered by the artificially of urban life. Not having consciously recognized his own objective, he could not know that the technology he used and his relationship to the guide prevented him from achieving that objective. His story is a compensation for not having satisfied a desire which he did not recognize or understand.

For our work to be satisfying, we need mobility and involvement with other people. Almost all spontaneous or "primitive" forms of work organization provide these but our technology makes it possible to eliminate mobility and human involvement for many office and factory workers. It is still not possible to place the same restriction on construction workers, but we are moving in that direction even there.

When workers' mobility and involvement opportunities are severely restricted, dissatisfaction is inevitable. It may manifest itself indirectly, as in unreasonable wage demands or shoddy work, but it will be there. As the technology we use influences, and at times, dictates our form of organization and therefore the degree of mobility and involvement, it merits serious consideration.

Scientific management, as proposed by Frederick Taylor, stressed the elimination of wasted effort and movement, to obtain maximum production from each worker. He advocated breaking jobs down into repetitive tasks which could be mastered quickly and be performed hour after hour without interruption. Assembly lines in factories and their counterparts in offices incorporate these principles. Despite more than ample evidence that scientific management does not produce the results expected by Taylor, let alone produce job satisfaction, the concept still has a strong influence on our thinking. Much of our modern technology is designed to permit wider application of the concept.

Twenty years ago most stenographers took dictation in shorthand. This required them to go to the office of the person dictating and return to their typewriter to transcribe the dictation. En route, they often delivered messages, performed incidental tasks and exchanged pleasantries with other workers. They were mobile and involved.

Ten years ago, dictation machines gained in popularity. Their appeal was based on eliminating wasted stenographers' time while the boss hummed and hawed or was interrupted by telephone calls or visitors. The stenographers could spend more time at their typewriters

— presumably working. Their mobility and involvement decreased and so did their ability to make a wider contribution.

Five years ago, centralized dictation systems gained in popularity in large offices. In those brave new offices, managers have intercom telephones hooked up to a room containing tape recorders and stenographers. The stenographers select recorded tapes, put on their headsets and type the words recorded by disembodied voices. No time is wasted walking or talking. Finished products are dispatched to the managers by an office boy. Mobility and involvement are almost eliminated. Managers in those offices frequently complain about the poor work done by the stenographers and blame it on the schools and the laziness of the younger generation. They fail to see that their technology dictated a form of organization that was bound to lead to poor workmanship.

Photocopy equipment has had a tremendous impact on offices during the past few years. Its relevance to this chapter comes from the fact that it reduces personal involvement in communications by increasing written communications.

Computers usually lead to a form of organization which isolates groups by craft and status and limits human contact to members of the groups.

Private offices often are symbols indicating that the occupant has achieved some kind of desirable status. But once achieved, the occupant regularly seeks excuses to leave his office — to be mobile, to mingle, to talk, to be involved with other people. Having reached the heights symbolized by his office, he can do this without being aware that the clerks and typists sitting at desks lined in neat rows have the same need for mobility and involvement. But again, technology dictates rows of desks while humanity dictates groupings.

We have a wide choice in the technology we can draw on to assist in the performance of most office jobs. We therefore have great flexibility in the organization of office manpower and in the layout of the office itself.

There is less flexibility in factories but not as little as is often assumed. Frequently, the task to be performed dictates the technology to be used and influences, but need not dictate, the form of organization.

The main restriction on flexibility is derived from the fact that most machines and equipment must be stationary and located logically in relation to the work being done. These fixed locations coupled with the tendency towards narrow job definitions, reduces the possibilities for mobility and involvement with co-workers. If material to be worked on comes to the workplace, instead of being brought there by the worker, mobility is further restricted. Assembly lines impose almost complete restriction.

The often criticized grimness of assembly line work is not just the result of the repetitive monotony of the tasks. Assembly line workers are tied to a specific workplace where they are passive receivers of material upon which they perform tasks at a rate determined by someone else. There is almost no opportunity for mobility or involvement until the whistle sounds for coffee break implying, "You now have 10 minutes to restore your humanity."

In the factory, as in the office, it is a mistake to build human organizations around machinery and equipment. It is a mistake because it is neither efficient nor humanitarian. We can be satisfied, productive workers only when we have the work relationships demanded by our humanity.

This is not a back to nature plea. On the contrary, it would be foolish not to take advantage of modern technology to satisfy our material needs. But it is equally foolish to allow technology to destroy our spiritual life.

Our approach to organization must begin with our spiritual or human needs. Our need for mobility, our need for human involvement, our need for informal relationships with our co-workers, our need for active participation in our work.

The only people who can create an organization that meets these needs are the people who are part of the organization, that is, the workers. There is no need for experts to tell the workers how to meet their needs. Whenever workers are free to determine how work should be done, they evolve a system which meets the needs. They do it because it is the natural or instinctive thing to do. A specific illustration of this is discussed in some detail in a later chapter on Norway.

Summary

When we use technology that restricts mobility and involvement, we increase dissatisfaction and alienation and do not achieve the intended objective. When the workers themselves make decisions on technological changes and related changes in organization they will avoid the errors made by managers and "experts".

chapter seven

quantitative management techniques

ARLY in the first world war, the Minister of Defence, Sam Hughes, laid plans for Canadian troops to set sail from Halifax to Britain in a blaze of glory. Unfortunately, the teetotalers' campaigns against "demon rum" had not fully prepared him for the mundane task of allocating men and material to ships. Some of the ships left port overloaded with men; others left overloaded with equipment. Still other ships left almost empty while a good bit of the equipment the troops were to use in Europe, remained on the docks in Halifax.

During the second world war, logistics became the concern of specialists who developed mathematical techniques that improved the chances of men, food and equipment coming together in the right places at the right times. Since then, the number of mathematical techniques used in business has greatly increased. They can be placed in three main groups:

Scheduling — techniques to aid in solving logistics problems.
Decision-making — techniques intended to reduce risk or uncertainty when making decisions influenced by many factors
Controlling — techniques intended to help determine if objectives are being met.

It is widely assumed that because the techniques are mathematical or quantitative, they are objective and neutral — neutral in the sense that they perform a specific function with no positive or negative spill-over. In fact, however, they are far from objective or neutral, and with the exception of scheduling techniques, there is almost always a strongly negative spill-over.

The most widely used of the mathematical scheduling techniques is PERT (Program Evaluation Review Technique) which made its first formal appearance in the U.S. Navy in the late 1950's. Informally, it has been used for thousands of years.

PERT is primarily a technique for scheduling a series of operations so as to accomplish an objective with minimum delay. Through a desire to eke out a final few minutes of sleep, most of us have perfected the schedule of operations that must be performed between rising and arriving at work. We learn, for example, to schedule the operations so that the coffee is ready when we have finished shaving. Experienced cooks schedule operations so that each part of the meal is available at the appropriate time.

Scheduling the operations involved in a large construction project or a complex production process with PERT is considerably more difficult than scheduling a meal but the principle is the same. However, neither PERT nor related queueing theories are entirely successful in complex production scheduling. Redundancy must be built in, in the form of an excess stock of raw materials to avoid idle machines, and excess machines to avoid long queues and production bottle necks.

A new production planning system, called Daproplan, was developed recently in Sweden. It uses a highly specialized computer and may offer significant advantages to large manufacturers.

Quantitative scheduling techniques are compatible with industrial democracy, providing the purely technical aspects of scheduling are not permitted to determine policy. Specifically, what we decide to do should not be predetermined by scheduling. Scheduling must be a tool that assists us in achieving our objectives.

We all use quantitative techniques to assist in decisions we make in daily living. We compare costs of competing products when deciding what to buy and we measure things to decide if they will fit. We would find it very difficult to function without at least a basic knowledge of arithmetic. Enterprises would find it almost impossible to function without drawing on more advanced mathematical concepts. No one would deny that numerical data are essential to rational decision making. But it is not rational to attempt to quantify human values.

The U.S. military has been enchanted by 'gaming theories' which are mathematical techniques intended to simulate reality and thereby help determine the outcome of events which may or may not happen. Their concern is with simulating battles, with the players in the game being the U.S., with all its military strength, and the opponent, usually ill-equipped peasants in South East Asia. Superior military equipment can be counted on to assure U.S. victories in the games. The difference between the games and the reality is explained by the impossibility of quantifying those human qualities that enable people to resist seemingly overwhelming power.

Gaming theories and simulation techniques are sometimes used to determine competitive strategy in private businesses although price-fixing and market sharing agreements are simpler and more effective. Herman Kahn of the Hudson Institute has created an impression of profound thought, by quantifying qualities with apparently random numbers. My concern at this time, is with the tendency to apply the same thinking to a decision-making technique usually termed 'cost benefit analysis'.

In its simplest form, a cost-benefit analysis is a listing of costs associated with a proposed course of action and comparing them with a list of the benefits to be derived from it. The difference in the total cost and total benefit indicates the net gain or loss to be expected from the action. There would be nothing sinister or disturbing about this were it not for the fact that the technique is now used to measure qualitative as well as quantitative costs and benefits. This is accomplished either by ignoring qualitative factors or by assigning them weights and treating them as quantitative factors.

The stupidity of this is so apparent that I would ignore the technique were it not for the fact that it has permeated our society and can hinder the development of industrial democracy. Academics enthralled with value-free analysis are merely incorporating prevailing values into their analyses, rather than questioning those values. Politicians who talk glibly about priorities and trade-offs are doing so to avoid important value questions. Technologists who support their proposals with cost-benefit analysis are often trying to justify their personal preferences by 'objective' figures.

Bureaucratic hierarchies create conditions that encourage cost-benefit analysis because of the problem junior managers have communicating directly with top management. To get a proposal considered at the top, a junior manager has to write down the 'cold hard facts.' Translated, that means, "Tell us what it means in dollars and cents." There is no room for words such as dignity, satisfaction, humanity, or comradeship unless they can be assigned a dollar value.

The first step to preventing the abuse which comes from quantifying qualities, is to recognize the danger in doing so; particularly when it is disguised as 'value-free' analysis. The second step is to eliminate the bureaucratic hierarchies.

The next category of quantitative management techniques mentioned, was controlling or checking results achieved against objectives. As this can have a strong negative spill-over of concern to socialists, I will deal with it at some length — first within a capitalist context and later within a socialist environment.

Several years ago I spent some months as a student in a teacher's college. The thing I noticed first was that the quality of teaching was lower than any I had encountered in public school, high school or university. This may seem a little strange since one would expect the best teachers to be training other teachers, but it is nevertheless a fact.

I have thought back to those months many times since and I now believe that there was something much more significant than the poor quality of the teaching. There was an assumption that all of us who were then teaching or about to enter teaching careers, were incompetent. As a result of that assumption, we were subjected to a variety of controls and ultimately to various tests to see if we could measure up to some predetermined minimum acceptable level of competence.

Most of us realized rather quickly that all that was required was for us to figure out the measurement formula and then provide the professors with what they expected. We had no trouble doing that and as a result had a good bit of spare time for more pleasant activities. One of my colleagues at that time took the whole thing seriously and spent all his leisure hours studying. He was the only person in our class who failed.

Managers tend to make the same kind of assumption of incompetence. They learn fairly early on in their management careers that responsibility for certain activities and results must be delegated to specific people. They also learn that control systems have to be used to make sure that these specific people have met their responsibilities and achieved the results required. It is when they begin to develop the control systems that they unconsciously assume that the people who are to be subjected to the control systems are incompetent. Rather than raising the bottom level of achievement, they lower the upper level, because the upper level is most adversely influenced by controls.

When managers think in terms of controls, they think in terms of developing an objective system for measuring results. When they do that they almost invariably run into a conflict of measuring short term and long term results.

A manager in a private enterprise may say to me, "Your job is to increase sales in this division by X% next year."

I can meet his objective by putting more money into advertising and other selling expenses, without regard to the effect on profits.

He realizes that I can do this so he may say to me, "Increase profits in this division by X% next year."

I can meet this objective by deferring costs through techniques such as building inventories which will enable more rapid delivery and thereby enable the sales force to increase sales, and in the short run, increase profits. Alternatively, I can cut costs where the effect will not be felt in the short run.

So he may try to give me full responsibility for setting my own objectives and meeting my objectives, but he still feels the need for control so he draws on one of the newer popular control systems.

The newer systems vary considerably but the underlying concept is common to many of them. In effect, they say to employees, "Set your own objectives, plan your own projects to meet those objectives, prepare your budget for your projects. When approved, you · are the master of your own fate. You will be judged by how well you meet those objectives which you established for yourself."

This seems to get around the problem of managers juggling affairs to meet externally imposed objectives. In fact, the opposite is true. A specific example will illustrate the problem.

A friend of mine has for several years held a senior position in a large enterprise. His job is to facilitate sales. He is not a salesman or sales manager and he never carries an order pad. He makes a valuable contribution to the enterprise because he has extensive contacts and technical knowledge that many people rely on.

Until recently my friend had a free hand and I'm sure no one doubted that he was a valuable employee even though no one could say what percentage of sales he had generated. Haphazard, perhaps, but it worked.

Recently, in a burst of enthusiasm for the panacea of modern management, the whole enterprise switched to a new control system. My friend, along with all other senior personnel, was going to be held accountable for his projects and expenditures. He would have to set his objectives, plan his projects and budget. Then the control system would measure his success or failure.

The objectives were simple: facilitate sales. How? Through a combination of technical knowledge and contacts. But that's too vague. It doesn't show the clear cause and effect relationship the system demands. Projects must be justified in terms of measurable action and results.

Okay, if that's what the system and the backroom whiz-kids demand, that's what they will get. His network of contacts can be used for personal as well as corporate benefit. When he hears that a customer in Halifax, Toronto or Vancouver is likely to be placing a large order with his company he flies out and has a discussion over lunch with the customer's key people.

Now the reports show: Action — Lunch and discussion with representative of X Corporation. Results — $100,000 order placed one week later.

Dishonest? Perhaps. But it wasn't my friend's idea to draw short-term cause and effect relationships.

When a control system with the implicit assumption of incompetence is imposed, the assumption becomes a self-fulfilling prophecy. The very fact that someone with authority has prophesied or forecast the need for controls will be proven or self-fulfilled by the response of the people subjected to the controls. Each one, to a greater or lesser extent, will either try to beat the controls or will make decisions designed primarily to put himself in the best light rather than making decisions that are in the best interest of achieving overall objectives.

Every system for measuring and controlling must be relatively simple or contain relatively few components in comparison with the operation of the human brain. Even the giant computers are incapable of co-relating information in the same way as people do. As an eminent thinker, John Kari, has stated "Computers provide answers — the human mind provides judgment".

When a scientist or businessman or anyone else uses his mind to quantify all data relevant to the solution of a problem, he uses his mind as a poor substitute for a computer. When he uses a computer for judgments, he uses it as a poor substitute for his mind. The Edsel was a model answer to a problem and a model tribute to the absence of judgment.

All control systems favour answers rather than judgment. It is therefore inevitable that they lower the upper level of achievement rather than raising the lower level.

A few people are unhampered by control systems. Usually those people have enough self-confidence to rely on their own judgment and/or they don't care if they lose their present jobs. Most of us, with mortgage payments to meet, feel the pressure to be cautious so we seek answers demanded by the control systems and shy away from judgments required for real accomplishments.

This problem has beeen recognized in several large organizations that have experimented with a variety of management control systems. The typical solution has been to attempt to free exceptional talent from restrictive controls while continuing to subject most employees to controls.

This solution inevitably leads to an artificial situation with 'think groups' operating freely in a controlled environment. If the think groups are concerned only with technical problems related to products, they can make some contribution. If they are concerned with organizational and human problems their contribution will be a negative one because of resentment towards their privileged status. Their relative freedom from controls reveals the assumption that the majority must be subject to controls.

Of course people do not always respond according to our assumptions or expectations but the phenomenon is common where a dependency relationship exists. It occurs most often between teachers and students, parents and children, manager and employees.

The behavioural school of management recognizes the relationship between expectations and performance. As that school has considerable influence in universities, it is safe to conclude that most MBA's are aware of the relationship. However, awareness of the relationship makes no difference because no matter how many hours of lectures and seminars are devoted to it, an equivalent number of hours are devoted to the study of control systems containing the implicit assumption of incompetence. The business administration graduate enters business with an awareness of human behaviour, motivation and all sorts of fine sounding, progressive ideas about people at work. At the same time, he comes to business fully equipped with quantitatively based management techniques that are directly contradictory to what he knows about people.

So long as he keeps these two sets of knowledge in separate compartments, he can happily carry on his schizophrenic business career. He may raise hell with the profit picture, but his record looks good.

We appear to be caught in a vicious circle comprising the need for control systems and the destructive effects of control systems. The way out of the circle is to re-examine the assumptions upon which the systems are built.

Cash control systems have been used ever since money replaced barter. The destructive effects which always seem to accompany the newer management control systems do not always accompany cash control systems although they sometimes do. Why the inconsistency?

If you ask me to look after your cash and tell me I have a free hand because you trust me, I will probably decline your offer. Mistakes are inevitable. The first time I report a cash shortage, you will accept it as an innocent mistake. So too with the second error. But the third?

I am left with no protection. The same internal controls which safeguard your cash also safeguard my reputation because they enable me to prove my innocence. Thus we have a mutual interest in cash controls and providing we both understand their purpose they are not destructive.

The key is mutual interest and understanding. That is always absent from the quantitative management control systems no matter how much time is spent explaining their purpose to employees. That is because our explanation does not include the assumption that the employees are incompetent. That assumption soon becomes apparent and causes employees to try to beat the system in ways indicated earlier.

Non-destructive cash controls assume the possibility of human error and attempt to reduce its harm to employer and employee. Destructive cash controls assume dishonesty and they are destructive because the assumption can become a self-fulfilling prophecy. In that sense, they are similar to quantitative controls which assume incompetence. That assumption also becomes a self-fulfilling prophecy.

The old adage that suggests people respond in the way you expect them to, applies if we recognize that our expectations are often in the form of implicit assumptions which are manifested by our actions even when we are unaware of the assumptions.

We are all familiar with supervisors and managers who work overtime on petty details night after night. They will tell you that it is easier to look after the details themselves rather than delegate them to their subordinates. This, they say, is because the subordinates can't be relied on to do things properly and their work would all have to be checked.

Those supervisors and managers are right. Their subordinates can't be relied on because they may respond according to expectations.

To summarize, let us review the origin of the problem.

(1) Quantitative control systems contain an implicit assumption of incompetence on the part of those subjected to controls.
(2) The assumption is a self-fulfilling prophecy because of the dependency relationship between employee and employer.
(3) Control systems must be relatively simple compared to the complexity of the human mind. They therefore favour answers over judgment.
(4) By favouring answers over judgment, the upper levels of ability are curtailed.
(5) Operating without quantitative control systems would lead to inefficiency or chaos.

Or would it?

The results of business activity are expressed quantitatively. There is a need to know volume and costs of production, inventories and sales. Innumerable other quantitative data are required to plan effectively. Effective planning with follow-through comparison against performance is the key to avoiding unnecessary waste. In that sense, the whole object of collecting the quantitative data is to establish a control system over things that can be measured quantitatively. Our problem occurs when we try to apply the same control over people as we do over things.

Perhaps our striving for integrated systems caused us to extend our quantitative control systems from things to people. We can avoid the destructive effects of quantitative control systems by confining their applications to things and allow human judgment to operate in assessing the performance of people.

It may be easier to visualize the application of this principle by considering how it would apply to evaluating the performance of a secretary.

A major part of most secretarial jobs is taking dictation, typing, filing, answering the phone and arranging trips, meetings, etc. All of those things can be assessed quantitatively as words per minute, number of sheets filed per day or number of arrangements made. When adjusted for error rate we produce an objective evaluation of the secretary's performance. But any connection between that evaluation and the true value of the secretary is little more than coincidental.

Assuming the secretary is competent in the exercise of her skills (and it doesn't take long to find out that) her real contribution is made by exercising judgment. If we were to try to measure that we would be in the absurd position of trying to measure the number of nuisance calls we didn't get or the number of problems we didn't hear about because they were handled before they reached us.

Judgment tells us when a secretary exercises judgment. No quantitative formula will do that.

If we restrict the application of quantitative control systems to things and allow human judgment to be used in evaluating people there is a risk of subjective evaluation being abused. This risk is, in fact, one of the reasons for emphasis on quantitative evaluations. The fact that there is no evidence that quantitative, or the so-called objective techniques have reduced abuse does not seem to have made any difference to their popularity for abuse is inherent in any system of autocratic management.

Support for industrial democracy assumes that most people, given an opportunity, are competent and trustworthy. If industrial democracy is to succeed, it is important to avoid imposing quantitative control systems which contain an implicit contrary assumption. As suggested in the chapter on Power and Authority, we must remove employees from their position at the centre of pressures and control systems and put the job at the centre.

Summary

Quantitative techniques for work scheduling are compatible with industrial democracy provided the techniques are not permitted to determine objectives.

Cost-benefit analysis should never be used where human or qualitative factors are involved. Qualitative factors cannot be quantified without distortion and most cost-benefit analysis give a misleading impression of objectivity.

Any quantitative control technique that applies to people is bound to have a negative spill-over. Quantitative control techniques are useful only when applied to things.

chapter eight

computers

ALTHOUGH computers impinge on our lives in many ways, most people have little understanding of their capabilities. For some, computers are the hope for freeing man from all labour; for others, they represent a threat to employment; still others see them as a symbol of a dehumanized society.

Computers are, in fact, neutral inanimate objects which, like dynamite, can be used creatively or destructively. To use them creatively, one does not have to be a computer expert, but an understanding of their potential and limitations is required.

There are two distinct types of computers — analog and digital. The word analog is derived from analogy and as that suggests, analog computers illustrate likeness or similarities. Speedometers are simple analog computers which illustrate speed on a dial. Thermometers and weighing scales are other examples of simple analog computers.

Speedometers, thermometers and scales are measuring devices and their analog principle can be extended to cause something to happen in accordance with what the devices measure. A speedometer can become a governor which cuts off the fuel flow at a predetermined speed. Thermometers become thermostats which turn furnaces on or off at predetermined temperatures. Scales can be set to play a recorded overweight announcement at a predetermined point.

When rapid or complex response is required, analog computers are equipped with electronic circuits. This increases their potential but does not change one of their fundamental characteristics — analog computers are built to perform specific functions. A thermostat can be set to react at various temperatures but it can't be set to record the speed of your car. Some analog computers perform complicated functions and within those functions there may be great flexibility but that does not change the fact that what they can do is predetermined when they are built. In this respect, they differ fundamentally from digital computers.

There are certain limitations of size and speed built into every digital computer, but within those limitations, what they can do depends upon what they are instructed to do. A digital computer can be instructed, or programmed, to calculate the most economic route for a highway and that same computer can be programmed to produce payroll records and dozens of other unrelated tasks.

It is digital computers (referred to hereafter as computers) that are the main subject of this chapter.

The mystique surrounding computers stems in part from the early misnomer 'electronic brains'. Although the term is seldom used now, the belief persists that computers are super-human brains, or, failing that, the people who program computers have super-human brains. This false belief has led many people to place great faith in answers produced by computers. To provide a more realistic starting point, I will attempt to give a simple explanation of the capabilities of computers.

Computers are able to follow a series of relatively simple instructions in the form of a program. The instructions enable a computer to perform arithmetic functions, place and remove data from its memory section and compare numbers to determine if one number is greater than, equal to, or less than another number. The results of comparisons can be used as the basis for choosing what part of the program should be executed next. This ability to compare and select from alternative, pre-programmed, sets of instructions is the extent of the logic ability of computers. The fantastic speed with which computers can make calculations, comparisons and choices gives a misleading impression of magic or brain-like ability.

The speed of computers enables them to perform calculations which would be too lengthy for humans to perform. That speed has made space flight and ICBM's possible.

The speed with which computers can draw information from massive electronic memory banks makes it possible for doctors to instantly obtain information useful in treating illness. That same ability makes it possible for police forces to instantly obtain information about millions of people.

Computer speed has introduced a new dimension into many activities. The change is not only quantitative but qualitative. If you have a car that will cruise at 80 m.p.h., you can drive from place to place more quickly than in a car with a maximum speed of 60 m.p.h. The change is mainly in the quantity of time while the essence of the activity remains the same. Computer speed, however, makes possible new activities and therefore a qualitative as well as quantitative change.

In a lecture entitled *The Triumph of Technology*: *"Can" Implies "Ought"*, Hasan Ozbekhan explained how we are driven by the dynamics of technology to the point where we feel that we ought to do a thing because we can do it. Put another way, part of our value system is determined by our technology.

Nowhere is this more apparent than with computers which have been used on many tasks with the sole justification that it was technically possible to do so. This had led to abuse, inefficiency and an uneconomic allocation of resources.

Within enterprises operated on democratic principles, ways must be found to take advantage of computers while preventing abuse and misallocation of resources. This can be done only if we recognize the 'can implies ought' trap and are determined to avoid it. The value question, 'Should we do it?' must precede the technical question, 'Can we do it?' Because we seldom ask value questions unless we assume technical feasibility, the sequence is often reversed and leads us into the trap. We do not ask, 'Should we grow wings and fly to Montreal?' because of the apparent technical impossibility.

In turning to the things which computers can do reasonably well, I am in no way implying that they ought to be done by computers in every enterprise.

We can classify the tasks that can be performed by computers into four main categories.

(1) Scientific and engineering calculations
(2) Processing of accounting and clerical data
(3) Information retrieval
(4) Coordination

The potential of computers is most exploited when they are used to perform complex scientific and engineering calculations. Calculations are performed electronically within computers and involve no mechanical movement. Speeds of a few millionths of a second per calculation are common. These speeds contrast sharply with the relative slowness involved in the mechanical operations of feeding data into computers or printing data out from computers. This relative slowness seldom hampers complex calculations as the use of mechanical input and output units is small compared with the use of the electronic units. In brief, a computer is at its best when you put a little bit of data into it and do a lot of work with the data once it's in there.

Although computers were originally designed primarily for high speed complex calculations, their potential as processors of accounting and clerical data soon became apparent. These tasks presented a problem as they required moving a lot of data into and out of the computer, while performing relatively simple calculations inside the computer. The electronic units were underemployed while waiting for the mechanical units to bring in, or put out, data. In an attempt to reduce this problem, numerous faster input and output devices have been developed. These can only reduce the discrepancy in mechanical and electronic speeds and never eliminate it. To further reduce the problem, complex systems have been developed to enable the electronic components to carry on with other tasks, while awaiting new data to be fed from the mechanical units.

Processing accounting data requires frequent reference to a mass of records of such things as accounts receivable, payable and inventories, so auxiliary memories or storage units have been developed. Retaining this mass within the computer memory is prohibitively expensive so auxiliary memories or storage units have been developed. These usually take the form of magnetic tapes or discs hooked up to the computer.

These developments (faster input/output devices, simultaneous processing systems and auxiliary memory banks) have added greatly to the cost of a basic computer. Although widely used, there is little reliable evidence that the high capital and operating costs can be offset by personnel or other savings, when computers are used by enterprises to process accounting and clerical data.

The development of auxiliary memory banks which can be quickly accessed by a computer, allows computers to be used for information retrieval tasks. Airline reservation systems are an example of this. Reservation clerks have terminals linked by telephone wires to a central computer which in turn is coupled to memory banks containing details of all planned flights. Almost instantly, clerks can find out what spaces are available and, as reservations are made, the memory banks are updated. Other tasks falling in the information retrieval category include maintenance of credit and police files.

The coordination category refers to scheduling the steps necessary to reach an objective. The value of computers in coordination is derived from their ability to correlate a mass of information. For example, the schedule for bringing together appropriate men, materials and equipment on large construction projects, is frequently planned by computers. Given that computers can perform a wide variety of tasks, we will consider what tasks computers should perform. Three factors must be considered:

(1) Direct costs
(2) Effect on job satisfaction
(3) Possible abuse

I will attempt to relate each of these considerations to the four categories of computer tasks discussed earlier.

Scientific and engineering calculations represent the easiest category to deal with. Comparing the direct costs of using, or not using, a computer on these tasks is fairly simple. Even if no direct saving results from computer use, the ability to complete tasks sooner, may weight the decision in favour of a computer. Job satisfaction is more likely to increase than to decrease, because a computer can free engineers and scientists to concentrate on projects where they can be most productive or creative. There is no significant danger of abuse in using computers this way.

It is much more difficult to decide if computers should be used to process accounting and clerical data. As indicated earlier, anticipated savings seldom materialize. In applications where direct costs have been reduced, the savings are often more than offset by increases in indirect costs arising from dissatisfaction and unforeseen problems.

Computers can be economically used on these tasks if:

(a) They are repetitious
(b) Volume is high
(c) Judgment is not required

Success is dependent upon all three criteria and attempts to justify computer use when one is absent, invariably lead to failure.

Once a computer is installed for a particular purpose, there is a strong temptation to gradually add all accounting and clerical routines. Many of these that do not meet the criteria above, are justified as steps towards a fully integrated system. Fully integrated systems bring together all data concerning an enterprise into a coherent whole. These systems exist only in the minds of computer programmers. The concept has a certain emotional appeal but we lack the expertise required to make it a reality. Even if we developed the necessary expertise, it could be used more effectively elsewhere.

Admirable as it may be to climb mountains because they are there, it is undesirable to carry the same philosophy over to computers. When computers are used to process accounting and clerical data, the operating costs are likely to be considerably greater than the capital costs.

When it appears that a task can be handled economically by a computer, the side effects, or indirect costs of doing so, should be examined.

It is widely assumed that computers reduce the number of repetitive, monotonous jobs. This assumption has some validity when analog computers are used to automate production machinery. When digital computers are used to automate accounting and clerical routines, the reverse may be true. As this can have a significant effect on organization structure, it merits further examination.

When accounting and clerical routines are processed manually (with the aid of office equipment such as typewriters, calculators, duplicators, etc.), the tasks performed range from the very simple to the very complex. The range of skills required form a continuum. Off to the side of the continuum are certain specialized skills, but these are comparatively few.

The continuum allows great flexibility in organizing office work. It can be (and frequently is) split up into dull, meaningless, repetitive tasks. Or it can be combined into varied, meaningful jobs.

The introduction of a computer breaks the hierarchy of skills. Upward mobility is restricted and flexibility in organization greatly reduced.

When a computer dominates office work, three distinct groups of employees emerge:

(1) Those concerned with preparing data to feed the computer. They include clerks who convert raw data from invoices, time cards etc., into a medium which can be read by the computer — most often, punched cards.
(2) Those concerned directly with the computer, including computer operators, coders, programmers and systems analysts.
(3) Those concerned with using information which has been processed by the computer, including managers and others involved in following up a variety of problems.

Within each of these groups there is limited mobility, but almost none between the groups.

Employees preparing data to feed computers use a limited range of skills for repetitious tasks. Although isolated from the computer operations, they are the scape-goats for errors in computer output.

Employees involved directly with the computer become, by the nature of their work, isolated from the objectives of the enterprise.

Managers and other employees dependent upon the computer output to resolve operational problems, often find their time devoted to resolving problems created by the computer. Not surprisingly, this can lead to illwill towards computer personnel.

These organizational problems, created by the installation of a computer, not only create dissatisfaction, they open the way for abuse. Power can be concentrated in the hands of those directly involved in the computer operation. Some techniques for overcoming these problems are discussed later.

Information retrieval applications can be justified economically only if the volume is great and high speed retrieval is essential. Such applications are unlikely to create major personnel problems but there can be a real danger of power flowing from the control of information. This was discussed earlier in the chapter on power and authority. Techniques for reducing the problem are discussed later.

It is difficult to determine the costs or savings arising from using computers in coordinating, as a number of coordination or scheduling techniques are simply not practical unless a computer is used. We can, therefore, only weigh direct costs of computer usage against possible indirect savings through better coordination. In considering effects on job satisfaction and possible abuse, we must consider not the computer itself, but the coordination techniques. Their potential for abuse is great and a separate chapter — Quantitative Management Techniques — has been devoted to them.

I outlined above the main categories of tasks often handled by computers and indicated the categories most open to abuse through concentration of power and worker dissatisfaction. The following comments outline techniques that will prevent, or limit, abuse.

Control over secret information is an effective tool for converting legitimate authority into personal power. Computer personnel are able to exercise control on two counts — first, they can claim exclusive mastery over the computing techniques and second, they hold the key to the information in the computer memory banks. In corporation after corporation, line managers with direct responsibility for production and distribution have become subservient to the corporate computers.

In enterprises operating on democratic principles, no person should be able to exercise authority which is not subject to challenge by employees. Authority not subject to challenge becomes power.

But useful challenge is possible only when the challenger has relevant information at his disposal. Political democracy functions only when it is possible for citizens to weigh alternatives and challenge those in authority. This is also a prerequisite of industrial democracy. If this prerequisite is to be met, all employees in enterprises using general purpose computers must have sufficient understanding of the computers to enable them to question the experts. This is not as difficult as it might appear.

With a few hours of instruction and study, most adults can acquire enough understanding of computers to appreciate their capabilities and limitations. Given that basic knowledge, computer specialists should be able to explain and justify their proposals for computer usage. Failure to do so indicates either that they are unwilling to do so or that no justification is possible. The smokescreen of technical jargon is used by computer specialists, and specialists in many other fields to disguise muddled thinking.

Perhaps 'disguise' is not the best word as it implies a conscious distortion of reality. Jargon is more often an unconscious substitution for clear thinking. Requiring specialists to express their ideas in simple language often helps them clarify their own thoughts. This, in itself, is worthwhile.

The importance of communication between specialists and non-specialists should not be overlooked. Every group of specialists tends to become ingrown and assume elitist characteristics. Their jargon expands and reality is lost sight of. Their specialized knowledge is useful only for writing articles in obscure periodicals read only, if at all, by their fellow specialists. They can no longer make a contribution to society because they look down on their colleagues who express their views in a language understandable to laymen. Like witch-doctors, their status depends upon being unintelligible.

In addition to open communication, structural changes are necessary to prevent abuse. The strategy suggested throughout this book is based on starting with organizational structures as they exist and modifying them at the upper levels, so that an evolutionary process leading to full industrial democracy will be facilitated.

In most large enterprises, general purpose computers are under the control of a separate data processing department. The head of the data processing department usually reports to a senior officer-controller, vice-president or president. He is seldom, if ever, accountable to line managers who are directly dependent upon information produced by the computer.

If the manager of the data processing department is, as is usually the case, an expert in computers, he should be replaced by a person familiar with, and experienced in, the main operations of the enterprise. This new person needs no more than a layman's understanding of computers but he must have had broad experience in this or similar enterprises and he must have an understanding of, and sympathy for, the concept of industrial democracy. Initially, he should be accountable to a committee of line managers whose departments are affected by the computer operations. As the process of industrial democracy continues, it should apply to that data processing department as well as to all other departments.

Summary

Computers have the potential to facilitate or inhibit the process of industrial democracy. To facilitate the process, workers must gain some understanding of computers and avoid using computers where they:

(a) fragmentize work
(b) create more meaningless tasks
(c) substitute for judgment

Positive steps must be taken to prevent an elitist group from controlling computers and information.

chapter nine

committees

THE word "committee" has an unfortunate, almost humourous connotation, partly attributable to the frequent reference to camels being
animals designed by a committee. Partly, the connotation arises from
widespread experience of ineffective committees. Success in industrial
democracy depends upon success with committees and their frequent
failures do not invalidate the concept.

Committees established as vehicles for deferring action, or to
create a phoney sense of participation, will be ineffective. There is a
correlation between responsibility for committee decisions and responsible behaviour by committee members. If you serve on a committee whose recommendations are regularly changed or disregarded by
some higher authority, it will just be a matter of time until you and
your fellow members shortcut serious discussion and research with the
comment, "What the hell, it doesn't matter anyway." But if you have
to live with your decisions, it does matter, and you will put in the
extra effort required to make the best decision. The relationship means
that committees operating within an authoritarian organization tend to
be ineffective and their recommendations will not represent a synthesis
of the best each member is able to contribute.

It takes time for a committee to make the transition from a collection of individuals to an effective group. When a committee consists of people not used to working with each other, progress is usually very slow. There is a tendency for the committee to get bogged down on minor points and it takes a few meetings before a proper working relationship and feeling of trust is established. When they are established, decisions can be made informally and quickly, often by almost casual conversation over coffee.

Japanese businesses provide an interesting variation in collective decision-making at the management level. Major questions are discussed with all managers who might be even remotely concerned about the matter. An attempt is made to reach a unanimous decision before it is committed to paper and circulated for each manager to affix his seal. If, during circulation, there is disagreement on some point, the issue is reopened and the process starts over again. When complete, the document goes to the corporation president for the formality of final approval.

This is an oversimplified account of the process known as "Ringi", but it is sufficient to illustrate what seems to be a very slow, roundabout way to make decisions. When I first became interested in the process, I found it difficult to reconcile its apparent inefficiency with the dynamic Japanese economy. I found the explanation through discussion with Dr. S. G. Harris, who, for several years, was Canada's trade commissioner in Japan.

An important part of Japanese culture, often described by westerners as "saving face", applies not just to preserving one's own status or dignity, but that of others as well. If one makes incorrect decisions, one loses face. If a collective decision is bad, all participants lose face. All participants in a Ringi are therefore committed to successful implementation of their collective decisions. As Dr. Harris commented, "When everyone is committed to making it work, even a half-baked idea will be successful." That common commitment is lacking when committees are used in most Canadian businesses.

Within our prevailing business management culture, one saves face by being right. When there are disagreements one proves his rightness by proving that others are wrong. Far from having a common commitment to successful implementation of committee decisions, those who opposed the decision save face by eventually being able to say, "I told you so." They gain by failure which they may help foster to prove their rightness. The damage to the corporation is incidental because most managers learn that the corporate ladder they are climbing is made of the bodies of their colleagues. They also learn to get credit for ideas by withholding them from committee meetings and presenting them directly to higher management. Chester Burger's books such as *Survival in the Executive Jungle* or *Executives Under Fire*, are amongst many books that illustrate this point.

I am not presenting Japanese practices as a model for Canada. The point I want to illustrate is that collective decisions can be effective, or they can be ineffective. When those making the decisions must live with the decisions, they have a common commitment to success, similar to that which occurs in Japan for cultural reasons. This commitment is both a prerequisite to and result of, industrial democracy.

As a prerequisite, it is something that must be encouraged during the early stages of transition from autocratic management to industrial democracy. As a result, it is something that will grow as people learn to work together within an enterprise they themselves control. The rewards for selfishness in private enterprise disappear in industrial democracy.

It would be naive to assume that industrial democracy will bring an end to disagreement and inter-personal conflict. Employees are not going to make collective decisions in meetings influenced only by the calm voice of reason. Lively, impassioned debate will be present even more so than now. But there is a fundamental difference in debate and conflict designed to produce a victor who is entitled to the largest share of the spoils, and debate designed to determine the best course of action to reach a common goal.

Summary

Widespread disillusionment with committees is not an indication that committees are inherently ineffective. Rather, it is an indication of the lack of desire to be effective and of the referral to committees of conflicts that cannot be resolved within autocratic organizations.

When there is a common objective and a desire to reach that objective, committees can be effective.

chapter ten

communication

THE origin escapes me, but I think it was in the early 1960's when it became popular to call many things communication problems. The popularity has grown ever since then and we are now told that the government must learn to communicate with the people, that union leaders must learn to communicate with their members, and that communication is the number one problem in business. To communicate my opinion of this caper, it is just a lot of bovine excrement covering up real problems. I would leave it at that were it not for the fact that use of the label can create the reality and interfere with the development of industrial democracy.

All animals, including man, have the ability to communicate. Dogs communicate the boundaries of their territories to other dogs in a manner unacceptable in 'polite' society. Rhinos accomplish the same thing with their defecation rings, also unacceptable in polite society but reminiscent of the delineation of department boundaries in business. Crows are remarkably effective in communicating with large flocks by using a variety of sounds. As most hunters know, red squirrels can communicate warnings to every bird or animal in hearing range. But we, with our sophisticated languages and advanced communications technology, talk about a communication problem.

When we have a genuine communication problem, it is because we have erected a communication barrier. The other things labelled as communication problems are just symptoms of conflicting interests.

When people complain about high unemployment, it is not because the government is unable to communicate an erroneous economic theory that demonstrates a need for unemployment. It is a straightforward conflict. Capitalist governments want to keep a pool of unemployed people in the country and the unemployed people want to work. No communication's miracle is going to bridge the gap.

When management and labour are $2 an hour apart at the bargaining table, it is not because they aren't communicating. Each side knows full well what the other side is saying. They just can't agree because their interests conflict.

The same is true within an enterprise among people who are presumed to have common interests. Written directives from top management to junior managers, supervisors and foremen are interpreted in many different ways. This is not necessarily because of a lack of clarity in the directives but more likely because of conflicting interests.

None of us is able to write more than a few words without those words being open to more than one possible interpretation and when we receive directives, we interpret them according to our own interests. While this is not always apparent at work, it is apparent in the courts. Legal statutes use ten words instead of one to prevent misinterpretation but judges spend much of their time listening to conflicting interpretations. Obviously, each party in a legal dispute wants to interpret the relevant statutes in his own interest. Directives from top management are much the same. Each person down the line has his own interest in making things easy for himself, furthering his own ambitions or doing the best job he can. He interprets directives in that light.

When we label conflicts as communication problems, we avoid facing up to the real problems. There are, however, some real communication problems caused by artificial barriers to communication.

The most effective communication usually takes place between people speaking face-to-face. When we speak directly to someone, we get immediate feedback in the form of questions or facial expressions. We instinctively adjust what we are saying, or how we are saying it, according to the feedback. Any barrier to immediate feedback, reduces the effectiveness of communication.

The major barriers to communication in enterprises are:

(1) Formal channels of communication
(2) Layers of management
(3) Technological communication aids

Formal channels of communication assume that a flow of information on predetermined topics can move in predetermined directions so that each person obtains the information he needs to do his job. The assumption is incorrect. To do his job, each person establishes his own informal channels of communication.

Channels of communication are usually formalized in enterprises with several layers of management. Information is expected to go up and down the hierarchy without bypassing any layers. (After all, it's not proper to go over your boss's head.) As information filters through each level it is screened, edited and interpreted so that the finished product may have only a faint resemblance to the original.

These points are fairly obvious and require little elaboration. Less obvious are the technological barriers to communication. They are less obviously barriers because they appear to be aids.

Telephones are an accepted part of our civilization and it would be ridiculous to attempt to operate an enterprise without both an external and internal telephone system. The convenience of phones is beyond dispute, but they are not a substitute for face-to-face communication. They provide an immediate voice feedback but the voice is not accompanied by facial expressions and gestures. It is, therefore, an incomplete communication which does not hold our attention.

Telephones are suitable for giving or receiving straight-forward factual information, but unsuitable for serious discussion or conveying ideas. When we are seduced by their convenience and use them when they are unsuitable, they become barriers to communication.

Public address systems in plants and offices are worse than useless. Employees either ignore P.A. announcements or resent them. It is a strictly one-way communication medium with a strong authoritarian connotation. Some kind of voice amplification system is required for speakers talking to large audiences, but P.A. systems are of no use in communicating with employees scattered throughout a building.

Photocopy machines have had a major impact on office communications and a lesser impact in factories. Their impact is a function of their convenience. Place the material you want copied in the machine, set the dial for the number of copies you want, press the start button and there you have it — copies for everyone with a few extras in case you forgot someone. Your pearls of wisdom can be reproduced and distributed thanks to modern communications technology. But the technology creates a true communication problem. There is no immediate feedback and unless you are a poet or a writer of inspirational prose, the message is cold and dehumanized.

The convenience of photocopy equipment often leads to written communication replacing face-to-face communication. The delay in feedback gives time for misunderstanding to become resentment and for resentment to become hardened opposition as interpretation speeds along the grapevine. And the grapevine is bound to be more credible than the photocopy because the grapevine operates on face-to-face communication.

Like telephone calls, written messages are fine for conveying straight-forward information, but when used as a substitute for face-to-face communication, they are a barrier between people and a cause of alienation.

Industrial democracy will not operate in a mass of written memos and directives — many of which are now written more to put things in the record than to communicate. Communication technology must become a servant to the democratic process instead of a barrier or substitute for face-to-face communication.

Noise is a different kind of barrier to communication and in most jobs where noise levels are too high to permit communication, a system of hand signals or signs develop. Some of these systems are elaborate. They go well beyond meeting the communication demands of the job and meet some of the demands for communication with people.

The major problem with noise is not that it is a barrier to communication, but that it permanently damages hearing. The solution to that problem does not lie in more or cheaper hearing aids.

We have the technical knowledge required to reduce industrial noise. Much of that knowledge is not used because decisions are made by managers concerned with profit and not by workers affected by the noise. Industrial democracy will change that and where the technical knowledge is not yet available socialist governments have a responsibility to support the necessary research to make it available.

Summary

Communication becomes a problem when we create the problem by imposing hierarchical, departmental and technological barriers between people. Because of the importance of communication to the process of industrial democracy, these barriers must be avoided.

chapter eleven

motivation

IN 'The Revolution of Hope', Erich Fromm wrote, "It is of vital importance to distinguish between a psychology that understands and aims at the well-being of man and a psychology that studies man as an object, with the aim of making him more useful for the technological society."

The job of managers in capitalist enterprises is to maximize profit. They have at their disposal certain resources — material and human. Subject to some constraints imposed by law, social pressure, or trade unions, they are free to use the resources as they see fit. To some extent, material and human resources are interchangeable. If a job can be done at a lower cost by machine power than by manpower, human resources are replaced by material resources. If a better machine is available, it replaces the old machine. If better manpower were available, it would replace the old manpower. But with people, you can't count on greater efficiency with each new model. The problem, for managers, is to get more out of the old model.

Coercion and the threat of starvation are no longer effective managerial weapons. Managers are now expected to instill in their subordinates a desire to give their all to their work. This has led to a search

77

for means to motivate employees and to endless theories of motivation. There are, in fact, many management professors who consider that the ability to motivate employees is the most important skill for a manager to possess. All texts I am aware of dealing with personnel, stress the importance of motivation.

Most writers on the subject begin by distinguishing between motivation (good) and manipulation (bad). Then, under the heading of motivation, they proceed to wrap up manipulation techniques in psychological jargon. The field of psychology they draw on, has, to paraphrase Fromm, the aim of making man more useful to business. To be fair, the texts are not all bad. One of the best, in that it does use psychology for understanding rather than manipulation, is *Personnel: The Human Problems of Management,* by G. Strauss and L. R. Sayles (Prentice Hall).

Implicit in motivation theories is the assumption that some external motivating force must be created by managers before employees will work. It is interesting that the assumption does not apply to me, the writer, otherwise I would not be writing, or to you, the reader, otherwise you would not be reading, but only to them, the mass of faceless ones who haven't joined our elite little group of self-motivated people. I am reluctant to accept any theory of human behaviour that applies to them, but not to you or me.

As human animals, we all have certain biological needs, including the need for food, shelter and some degree of comfort. Every society has some form of organization to help meet those needs. As humans, we all have certain psychological needs, including what I will call for the moment, the need for recognition.

Our biological or physical needs not only motivate us to work, they force most of us to do at least a minimal amount of work. When we have met our basic needs, we may be motivated to do more work so we can eat better food, have more comforts and acquire more material possessions. These, however, are not universal needs, but learned needs and vary from person to person and from culture to culture. Each society tends to reinforce its learned needs by relating its system of rewards and punishments to them but in each society there are some people who will not accept what society says they need. In North America, for example, many people have rejected the belief that they need to be competitive, materialistic, acquisitive beings. Those who have not rejected that belief can be manipulated (or motivated) by managers who play on the employees' acquisitive desires. Incentive, or piece-work wages are one of the most common techniques for doing this. Their destructive effects are discussed in more detail elsewhere in this book.

Manipulative techniques that play on the psychological need for recognition are even more destructive. The following is a partial list of devices which can be used to play on this need. The list first appeared

in an insurance trade magazine and was later reprinted in a management
text as a guide for future managers.

Merit and performance rating
Salary increases
Promotional opportunities
Personal publicity
Seniority privileges
Various status symbols
Praise

The same techniques are recommended in more subtle form in
much managerial literature. It is therefore worth examining the need for
recognition.

If recognition is truly a need, it must apply to everyone and be a
prerequisite to survival. Otherwise it is just a widespread desire —
something most of us would like but can get along without.

Some psychologists define the need for recognition as a need for
acceptance by some social group and equate it with implicit or explicit
acclaim or praise. We know, however, that this is not a universal
requirement. Some people can live as hermits or devote their lives to
causes accepted by no other person. When we go beyond the super-
ficially slick psychological theories into the great philosophies and religions, we find a recurring theme that may also be described as a need
for recognition. But there it takes on a new meaning of self-recognition
or personal dignity or the knowledge of one's worthiness as a person.
This is truly a universal need for survival. Its absence leads to self-
destruction just as surely as does the absence of food and shelter.

Our need for self-recognition or dignity, manifests itself in various
ways because we are often not aware of what the need is. Even when
the need is recognized and understood, few people can maintain their
sense of inner dignity and worthiness without some reinforcement from
outside. Consciously, or unconsciously, we may seek this reinforcement
by doing things, or acquiring things that can be used for public display
of our worthiness. The things we do, or acquire, to prove our worthiness,
depend upon the prevailing values. We will reject the prevailing value
system if we have confidence in our own worthiness or, at the other
extreme, if we have no confidence in our ability to 'make good' within
the system.

If a lack of confidence in our ability to 'make good' in the prevailing
value system causes us to reject it, we seek to reinforce our sense of
worthiness by becoming part of a sub-system where we will be accepted
as equals instead of inferiors. So it is that insecure children from middle-
class suburban homes, may leave the competitive system in favour of
the drug route. For most children born in the slums, the attempts to
enter the main system entail too much risk to personal dignity. Poor
children learn early that their dignity is reinforced through acceptance
by other poor people, but it is damaged when they are treated as
inferiors while competing against near-impossible odds to enter the

middle class. Unless a poor child has a sufficiently strong sense of his own dignity to survive without external reinforcement, he will narrow his horizons to the world he knows and remain as part of the poverty cycle.

Most of us fall between the extremes of the saint whose survival is possible because of his sense of inner dignity, and the man who narrows his horizons to avoid loss of dignity through failure in the system. As socialists and humanists, we are concerned with creating an environment that enables more people to move along the continuum towards the saints. Motivation techniques based on our need for external reinforcement of our sense of dignity, tend to move us in the other direction along the continuum.

Where, then, does this leave managers during the transition stage from autocratic management to industrial democracy? The answer lies in an examination of factors that tend to demotivate or frustrate our natural desire to find satisfaction in our work.

Some of us are fortunate in having a reasonable choice of jobs open to us. We are not forced to take and stay at any available job in order to survive. We have some freedom to accept positions that interest us and reject those that do not. We therefore bring to a new job, a strong desire to do it well and we approach the new job with pleasant anticipation. This strong inner motivation can be destroyed by demotivators or frustrations. Socialist managers have a responsibility to reduce the chance of that happening.

Unnecessarily uncomfortable working conditions reduce natural motivation. Comfortable working conditions neutralize it but do not stimulate people to work harder. Similarly, poorly prepared food in the company cafeteria will reduce motivation but good food just neutralizes it. This is partly because unnecessary discomfort indicates management's contempt for the employees whereas the absence of unnecessary discomfort is to be expected. The key word is 'unnecessary'. Employees will tolerate hot, overcrowded working conditions without becoming discouraged, so long as there is no reasonable alternative accommodation available. When those same employees move into a modern, spacious building, they will become angered by failures in the air conditioning system and by all annoyances caused by poor planning of the building. This reaction takes place because there was an alternative to the inconveniences and discomforts and as the alternative was not chosen, it is a reflection of a contemptuous attitude.

The strongest demotivators are conditions that prevent employees from doing their jobs to the best of their abilities. Faced with such conditions, most people will keep struggling for a considerable time. Eventually, they will give up and get out, or reconcile themselves to the mediocre performance expected of them, or try to use the organization for personal gain.

Restrictive conditions exist in all large bureaucratic organizations. The more levels there are in the management hierarchy, the more likely are the chances of the restrictions being strong demotivators, because decisions regarding how jobs should be done are made by managers far removed from the people who have to do the jobs. The bureaucrats cannot demand excellence so they legislate mediocrity. To attempt to rise above the prescribed performance level is to be a trouble-maker and misfit.

The demotivational effects of conditions that prevent employees from using their abilities, cannot be offset by other devices or rewards, because the opportunity to fully use one's abilities is an essential part of job satisfaction. That opportunity will not exist so long as decisions about how jobs are to be done are made by people other than those doing the jobs. (This, of course, does not preclude the use of technical advisors.)

High on the list of priorities for socialist managers, is the need to shift responsibility for the way jobs are performed, to the employees doing the jobs. When that is accomplished, a good many motivation problems will disappear and a step will have been taken along the road to industrial democracy.

Summary

Most motivation theories used in business are destructive techniques for manipulating employees and have no place in industrial democracy. Instead of motivation theories, we must be careful to avoid those things which destroy inherent motivation.

chapter twelve

incentive wages

TRADE unionists and socialists usually have a philosophical objection to the use of piece-work and similar incentive wage plans that attempt to directly relate individual earnings to individual production. It is, however, not unknown for persons who object to them to be seduced by them. For this reason, I propose to illustrate, on pragmatic grounds, that incentive wage plans are, in the long run, counterproductive. For ease of illustration, let us consider the operation of incentive wage plans in privately owned industry where management's objective is to maximize profit.

First, the seductive aspects.

From management's point of view, production-tied wages appear to offer the following attractions:

(1) Incentive for employees to work harder.
(2) Ability to predetermine the labour element in production costs.
(3) Assurance that the cost of labour will be less than its value to the company.

From the employees' point of view, the attraction lies in the opportunity to increase earnings through individual effort.

Thus, there appears to be an advantage to both management and labour. The advantage, however, is, illusory on both sides.

For piece rates to be workable at all, production norms must be established. The rates must be such that normal production provides wages in line with prevailing rates in the industry. Above normal production must provide above normal wage rates. Before the plan gets past this stage there is a conflict of interest between management and labour.

It is in the interest of management to set the production norms as high as possible and in the interest of labour to set them as low as possible. If labour's interests prevail, it will result in a temporary increase in wages above going rates, but that will be offset in the next round of negotiations. Assuming that a reasonable compromise is agreed upon, we can turn to the next set of problems.

There are very few production processes in which the amount produced is entirely dependent upon the skill of the employees. Machines break down and materials are not always available when required. Employees are unlikely to accept an incentive pay system that penalizes them for production losses that are beyond their control, so an elaborate agreement must be worked out to distinguish between avoidable and non-avoidable production delays. The converse also applies. When productivity is increased by the use of better machinery, management will insist on changing the production norms. No agreement which simply states that $X will be paid per unit produced, will be workable.

If a workable agreement is arrived at, an elaborate system of records must be maintained in order to determine wages. This is an integral part of the cost of any piece-work pay system.

By their very nature, piece-work wages promote quantity over quality. To counteract this, inspection must be detailed and the cost of maintaining quality control will increase.

Assuming that the difficulties enumerated so far can be resolved, a temporary increase in productivity can be expected. Then one of two things (or perhaps a combination of them) will happen.

If the scheme works, in that it leads to an all-out effort by individuals to increase production, it will also lead to dog-eat-dog competition in the plant. Each employee will concentrate on those things that increase his own income. When possible, he will pass preventative maintainance on to the next shift rather than cut into his own production. He will use all avenues open to him to increase his own earnings at the expense of his co-workers. Inevitably, this will create problems which will work against the interests of both management and labour.

There is a more likely alternative because labour tends to be more realistic than management when it comes to assessing the effects of piece-work wages. This alternative is based on informal agreement on production norms by the employees and it has the effect of negating the apparent advantages of piece-work wages. This informal agreement, or understanding, usually evolves through lunch hour and coffee break discussions. The production norms so established provide an acceptable income for less than an all-out effort. The worker with average skill is able to hold his own with the highly skilled and the danger of rate cuts and layoffs arising from high productivity is reduced.

When an understanding on production norms is reached, group pressure works to force employees to conform to them. Any employee who consistently surpasses the group norms, may be popular with management but he will have difficulty with his co-workers and may find that his efforts are sabotaged by them.

Management, of course, objects to these informal agreements on production norms because they defeat the purpose of piece-work schemes. Even so, they are less harmful to management than the dog-eat-dog alternative although their existence means that the expensive record keeping and quality control procedures are just a waste of money.

None of this is original. These points appear frequently (sugar coated) in management literature, but as management literature has little influence on management, incentive pay systems still have appeal. Periodically, there are suggestions of 'merit pay' for teachers, which is just an extension of the piece-work concept. It would be interesting to see a merit pay formula that didn't cause even more distortion of formal education.

Salesmen are frequently on straight commission which is piece-work wages in its purest form. If piece-work wages are appropriate anywhere it is with salesmen. Commission can be calculated simply by multiplying rate times amount sold and the problems that arise in factories are not so obviously present in a sales force. In addition, salesmen who travel cannot be subjected to close supervision so they are expected to produce in order to increase their earnings.

Even here, with apparently ideal conditions, piece-work wages do not achieve their objective. Insofar as commissions do increase sales, they do so by overselling, often against the long-term interests of the enterprise, and at the cost of an overabundance of ulcers and heart attacks.

Salesmen do have, or should have, a useful function when handling complex products whose uses may not be apparent. That function is to assist potential users to obtain the most suitable product for their needs. It is primarily an educational function and is bound to be distorted when the salesman's earnings depend not upon how well he performs his function, but upon how much he sells.

So much for incentive wages. But how can we determine how much employees *should* be paid? Now there is a profound question. Too profound to be dealt with in a pedantic style so I will attempt to deal with it in a more human way.

Do you spend your time complaining because you are paid too much? I don't either. It's always other people who are overpaid while we are underpaid. It's strange that this should be so. Are we more deserving than they, or could it be that we are not quite logical?

Governments, companies, unions, economists, and professors throughout the world have searched for a logical formula to tell them how much salaries and wages should be. This is much like searching for a logical formula to tell you if you like vanilla ice cream better than chocolate cake. It may be an amusing pastime but it is not likely to lead to any great discoveries. Sweden, with its nationwide bargaining, has had the most notable success in formula finding, but the best that can be said for it is not that it is logical but that it works.

The formula finding game often starts by stating that people should be paid according to the value of the work they do. Students of metaphysics and others who speculate on the number of angels that can stand on the head of a pin, can go a long way with this starting point. The other experts soon find that there is no way to determine the value of work done by teachers, clergymen, doctors or truck drivers. If that problem were ever solved they would then have the job of figuring out the value of the labour of those who are figuring out the value of other people's labour. And so on, and on, and on.

When it becomes clear that there is no way out of this circle, those who play the game come to the conclusion that they must have a new starting point.

There are an unlimited number of starting points that could be used but professors, economists and government officials usually agree to use educational qualifications. They decide that if more education is required to be an employee in Group A than in Group B, then employees in Group A should be paid more. As most of the professors, economists and government officials have many years of formal education this happens to be a profitable way to look at things.

If you make a living in front of a blast furnace or by having your guts churned up while holding a pneumatic drill, you might wonder why people who enjoy the pleasures of a better education and plush offices should be higher paid as well. You might think that it would be a good idea to change our starting point so that we are paid according to the difficulty of the job we do. The argument that the person who works hardest should be paid most, has a nice ring to it. But it is impossible to apply. The hardest work I have ever done was during a summer I spent as a lumberjack. On the other hand, many good lumberjacks find their own work easier than they would mine which consists of talking, reading, writing and general messing around in an office. So who is to say which job is hardest?

Some people feel that dangerous work should be the highest paid. People who feel this way are usually the ones doing the dangerous jobs while the rest of us admire them from afar. But once again, how do we rate a job as dangerous?

I worked with a college student during my brief career as a lumberjack. When he had an axe in his hand, he made the job not only dangerous to himself but positively menacing to anyone within several feet of him. This was apparent when he missed a tree with a wild chop and his axe blade skimmed through the hat worn by the lumberjack working behind him. After the student received some colourful advice from the then hatless lumberjack, he was allowed to work alone until he sunk his axe into his own boot. As his foot was in his boot at the time, he was removed from the scene. Who should receive danger pay in these circumstances — the student or his co-workers?

Some companies develop formulas combining twenty or thirty factors such as education, danger, difficulty, working conditions and anything else which they think should influence pay. With such a formula, the boss can show us why we are paid less than the man at the next desk or machine. But this won't make us any happier as we judge our own pay in comparison with other people or groups.

If we were to compare our pay to that of our counterparts in India, most of us would seem to be pretty well off. But in India a small national pie has to shared out to a few hundred million people. We are more concerned to get a hefty slice of the large Canadian pie.

This really is what the game is all about. If you are among those who write the rules for the game, you get a good slice. If you are part of an organization strong enough to make its own rules, you get a good slice. If you are on the sidelines wondering what the rules are, don't worry too much. When the pie is sliced up there will be something left for you and there will be someone with a formula to prove you got just what you deserved.

I trust this diversion illustrates the impossibility of providing an objective answer to the question of wage determination. The total amount available for wages can be calculated more or less objectively once capital investment decisions are made, but no objective formula can determine wage differentials. As a socialist, I favour reducing the differentials to an absolute minimum. As Ian Adams and the three other writers of "The REAL Poverty Report" point out, "Talent is a nice thing to have. But it should not necessarily make its possessor rich. There is no reason why people should have to be rewarded with enormous affluence in order for them to make full use of their talents." They go on to state that ". . . Sweden has both more wage equality and an economy that grows faster than ours. Efficiency does not depend on inequality unless the Swedes are cooking their books."

Wage inequalities cannot be eliminated overnight, but their elimination must be an objective of socialists. The following suggestions are intended to chart a course towards that objective.

In our competitive, materialistic society, our 'success' is often judged by our incomes. We learn early that it is good to get ahead. But get ahead of whom? That is a question we are not supposed to ask. We may ask why we should get ahead because there is an obvious answer — to make more money — but when we ask who we should get ahead of it is more awkward to answer. It forces us to recognize that our success is dependent upon the failure of others. Recognition of this is not a solution to the problem of determining wages in democratic enterprises, but it is prerequisite to a solution.

There is another important factor that drives us to seek ever higher incomes. The cost of necessities such as food, housing, dental care, college education and transportation is so high that luxuries such as an annual three-week family vacation in a pleasant relaxing setting, are available only to those who got ahead.

The cost of necessities to individuals can be reduced by government action without increasing the cost to the country as a whole. Individuals do not pay directly to go to public school or to use parks, streets or hospitals. The same principle of spreading these costs can be extended to dental care, college education and public transportation. Good free or low cost public transportation would not only solve a number of environmental problems, it would also remove automobiles from necessities to luxuries. We are capable of producing and delivering basic foods to consumers at a very low cost. We can bring basic housing costs down to 10% or less of incomes.

Reduction of the cost of necessities has been a constant theme in the programs of socialist parties. The details of the economics involved is beyond the scope of this book except to say that it is practical in economic terms. My concern, here, is with its relevance to wages and industrial democracy.

When the cost of necessities is low, we have greater freedom to choose our work according to our interests and abilities. We are better able to view work as a satisfying activity rather than drive for survival and prestige. Satisfying work reduces the drive for consumption which now is often used to compensate for work alienation. The drive for consumption reinforces the need for more money. When we are able to overcome alienation, the cultural problem of relating income to success will be reduced.

These comments just touch on the political process which must accompany the full development of industrial democracy. Let us return to the immediate problem of the transitional stage within an enterprise.

We must begin where we are. In most medium sized corporations, pay at the top levels of management will often be at least 10 times as high as the pay for most employees. In addition, those at the top may receive fringe benefits worth as much as, or more than their salaries. Between the bottom and top are supervisors, middle managers and specialists, often well paid, but seldom receiving the stock options and other fringe benefits enjoyed by senior managers.

These large pay differentials are not compatible with industrial democracy. They can be avoided when a new enterprise is developed but they present a problem when we attempt to convert an established enterprise. Most people make commitments close to the limits of their incomes even when those incomes are in the $50,000 to $70,000 range. A sudden reduction would create hardship for innocent people unless time were allowed to plan for change in income or place of employment. We should aim, therefore, towards a phasing out of highly paid positions with the benefits being passed down to the bottom in order to narrow the gap.

As old management positions are phased out and new co-ordinators are elected by the workers, a fundamental change must be made in order to prevent a new hierarchy from becoming entrenched. The rate of pay for coordinators should be the same as the rate of the people whose work is being coordinated. An additional allowance can be paid to coordinators during the term of office, to compensate for extra hours involved in meetings, but it is important that it be a temporary allowance so that there is no hardship or stigma attached to replacing a coordinator.

The allowance need not be large to attract the right coordinators and if it is large, it may attract the wrong coordinators — those who seek the kind of power and prestige that alienates. The skills required by coordinators (or managers) are not rare although most work environments suppress them so they appear to be rare. Nor are those skills superior to the skills required to do any job well so there is no need to offer inequitable financial rewards to those who possess them.

There are, however, some skills that are rare and essential to many enterprises. For the foreseeable future, these will lead to wage inequalities. This should not create major problems. It doesn't matter too much if the engineer who designs a product earns more than the machinists who produce the product, providing that the machinists earn a reasonable wage and providing the engineer is not their boss.

A sequence of events leading to a wage structure compatible with industrial democracy could be as follows:

(1) Raise lower pay rates so that every employee earns enough for a reasonable standard of living. This will more likely come through a change in legal minimum wages rather than within each enterprise individually.
(2) Move out all senior executives (president and vice-president levels). To avoid unnecessary hardship, this move can be done by a combination of early retirements, sabbatical leaves and appointments to enterprise advisory boards. The advisory boards can be useful providing they are limited to giving advice. Their salaries, but not their fringe benefits, can be carried on for several years or until they can adapt to alternative and more productive employment. As with all workers, former senior executives should have access to retraining programs.
(3) Foremen, supervisors and department managers should have a choice of seeking election as coordinators or joining the ranks of the workers. Either way, their salaries should be maintained at their former level until their fellow workers reach that level.

Beyond this point it is impossible to predict the events which will lead to a more equitable pay structure because at this point, industrial democracy will begin to function. We can, however, predict that as the workers move closer to self-management, and the former management system becomes redundant, present inequities will not be tolerated. Pay formulas will likely vary from one enterprise to another with supply and demand gradually giving way to the socialist concept of 'from each according to his means, to each according to his needs'.

Summary

Incentive or piece-work wages are counter-productive. There is no objective formula for determining what wages or wage differential should be. Socialists, however, strive to reduce differentials. More equitable wages is one of the outcomes of industrial democracy, partly because it follows logically from a commitment to industrial democracy and partly because the reduction in alienation leads to a reduction in the desire to own more and more things.

The move towards more equitable wage systems can be facilitated by action that reduces the cost of necessities.

chapter thirteen

profit

O NE of the yardsticks for measuring the success of enterprises is profit. In private enterprises, it is the most significant yardstick. In public enterprises, it may be the most significant or it may be incidental, but it is used. The word profit is like music to the ears of many capitalists. To many socialists it is closer to the sound of fingernails scratching a blackboard. It is a word used by everyone but understood by very few because it is an abstract accounting concept having, at most, an incidental connection with cash. This was aptly expressed by Howard Ross, a past president of the Canadian Institute of Chartered Accountants. In his book, "The Elusive Art of Accounting" (Ronald Press), Mr. Ross stated, "What financial statements describe as 'net income' (profit) is not really net income in the sense in which anyone but an accountant would understand the term. For one thing, the accountants' 'net income' is a figure arrived at after the systematic writing-off (or amortization) of expenditures made long ago that have absolutely no current relevance to anyone but an accountant."

One further quotation will illustrate the difficulty of understanding what profit is. "Arriving at an estimate of the periodic income of a business enterprise is perhaps the foremost objective of the accounting process. The word *estimate* is unfortunately proper because income is one of the most elusive concepts in the business and economic world. The art of accounting has not yet progressed (and never will) to the point where periodic income can be measured with certainty." (Intermediate Accounting: Meigs, Johnson et. al., McGraw-Hill.)

Both of these quotations are taken from books written several years ago but they are equally valid today. The problems do not occur because accountants are determined to hide facts but because they must draw artificial lines in order to make their task possible.

The first set of lines delineates a period of time. The accountants then attempt to report profits earned in that time period even though many transactions that took place earlier affect operations in that period and many transactions in that period will affect future time periods.

Another set of lines delineate the boundaries beyond which transactions have no recorded effect. Thus accountants record the cost to an enterprise of disposing of its effluence, but not the cost of environmental damage caused by disposal. Costs of hiring, paying and firing employees are recorded, but not the cost society must meet when employees cease to be employed.

Some accountants are anxious to push the boundaries further out and it is theoretically possible to do so. But to do so would add to the complexity of accounting and contribute very little useful information that could not be obtained more easily in other ways.

Within the boundaries of the enterprise is a matrix establishing a series of sub-boundaries. These are required in order to establish the revenues and costs associated with specific products, districts or activities and thereby determine their contribution to the enterprise.

Assume, for example, an enterprise produces two unrelated products such as chairs and ballpoint pens. Although some administrative and overhead costs will be common to both products, a reasonable allocation can be made and the contribution to the enterprise can be determined separately for each. Add related product lines using some of the same moulds or machines in the manufacturing process and the problem of allocating costs to specific products becomes more complex and more arbitrary. By-products, such as marketable shavings produced as an incidental to planing lumber, introduce another problem. Do they come free and yield a 100% profit when sold? Do they reduce the cost of the primary product by their yield? Or should some of the cost of producing the primary product be allocated to the by-product even though we cannot prevent the production of the by-product? The right answer is whatever we agree is the right answer.

Joint-products differ from by-products in that there is an intention to produce more than one product through a common process. We do not grow and slaughter cattle just for T-bone steaks even though they command a higher price than hamburger or pot roasts. All are joint-products of a single process and allocating cost to steaks and hamburger is arbitrary.

Accounting has two main functions; first to control the assets of enterprises and second, to provide information to show what has happened and to aid in planning what will happen. It performs these functions well, providing its limitations are recognized.

Published financial statements, which represent the culmination of the accounting process, are not intelligible unless the reader knows the rules and customs followed by accountants. A layman might look at a balance sheet and assume that the figures shown for the various assets represent their values. They do not. Some assets are shown at current values, some at estimated net realizable values, some at historical costs and some at cost less estimated amortization or depreciation. Some things under the asset heading may not be assets at all. Opportunity costs, imputed interest and changing dollar values are not reflected in most financial statements. As the amount of profit shown depends, in part, on the valuation of assets, the profit figure is also a mixture of apples and oranges.

With all their limitations, financial statements and profit figures are useful in comparisons and in detecting trends. Accountants follow certain accounting valuation principles consistently and if a valuation method has been changed in the period covered by a statement, the effect of the change will be shown. This enables useful comparison of similar enterprises and trends in specific enterprises, even though the figures, as absolutes, are not very significant.

Economic planning requires some measure of effectiveness of enterprises. Profit is one such measure, but is only one, and it is subject to severe limitations and is dangerous when used beyond its limitations. In particular, profit is so often used as a synonym for success that even socialists tend to use it that way.

When T. C. Douglas led the Saskatchewan CCF Government from 1944 to 1960, several new crown corporations were established. Taken as a whole, those corporations yielded substantial profits although the Liberal opposition did its best to discredit them by singling out examples of crown corporations that incurred losses. Some C.C.F. spokesmen defended the corporations on the grounds that they were profitable and attempted to demonstrate that the Liberals were misleading the public. Actually, the fact that the C.C.F were technically right and the Liberals technically wrong, was irrelevant as both sides were attempting to influence voters on the assumption that profit is a 'good thing'. It is not. It is neither a measure of success nor a measure of the extent of the exploitation of labour. It is, as indicated above, just an abstract accounting concept. For example, profitable companies can and do go bankrupt and other profitable companies represent a net loss to society. About all that can accurately be said about a profitable crown corporation is that it doesn't require direct subsidies from public funds. Thus Polymer Corp., which is profitable, is not directly subsidized, but the C.B.C. is because it is not profitable. However, Polymer is subsidized indirectly because it depends upon the infra-structure of transportation and trained and educated employees paid for by taxes, whereas the C.B.C. contributes to that infra-structure.

The Polymer profits and the C.B.C. losses do not indicate that Polymer is efficient and the C.B.C. inefficient. Nor do they indicate that Polymer makes a greater contribution to the Canadian economy than does the C.B.C. If the boundaries of accounting were expanded to include indirect subsidies and costs of environmental damage, we might find Polymer has been operating at a loss. That, however, would have little or no influence on our opinion of the rightness or wrongness of allocating resources to these corporations by direct or indirect subsidies. We may refer to the profit or loss figures to support out positions, but this is just a debating trick, or a rationalization, and is not what determines our opinions.

Conservative opposition to the C.B.C. is not because of the losses but because of its relative freedom from commercial constraints. Socialists support the C.B.C. because its programs are not completely commercialized. Liberal pragmatism is just an excuse to test the direction of the political winds and the pressure put on the C.B.C. by the governments, in the late 1960's and early 1970's, to obtain more advertising revenue, was not to reduce losses but to increase commercial influence on programs.

Similarly, the ultimate fate of Polymer will not be determined by its profitability. There has been pressure from Conservatives to sell Polymer to private investors, and pressure from New Democrats to keep it as a crown corporation. The Liberals have attempted to meet the Conservative objective and the New Democrat argument, by transferring Polymer to the Canada Development Corporation.

This diversion should be sufficient to illustrate that we don't use profit or loss figures to make rational decisions, but to rationalize our decisions. This does not imply criticism of how we make decisions for it would be unreasonable to attach too much importance to the figures summarized by the very limited art of accounting. Nor does this imply criticism of the accounting profession (of which I am a member) for we cannot produce figures about things that will enable others to make decisions about people. People is what the process of industrial democracy is all about and we must be careful not to equate the welfare of people with that abstract concept called profit.

Summary

Profits indicated on financial statements prepared by accountants are the result of calculations based on abstract concepts. The accountants' statements are useful in a limited way. It is important to recognize the limitations and not use them to make judgments beyond their limitations.

chapter fourteen

discipline

O NE of the rights of manager-bosses is to discipline employees for a variety of sins of omission or commission. This right has been so frequently abused that it is now limited by law and collective agreements. In non-unionized companies, even faulty grievance procedures tend to cause managers to be cautious in disciplining employees. But the right itself is not challenged, so the question arises of who would exercise that right if the manager-employee relationship were replaced by industrial democracy. Even though the question arises from an incorrect premise, it cannot be ignored.

Children are 'trained' by a system of rewards and punishments. Good behaviour is rewarded by parents and teachers. Bad behaviour is punished by them. What is good and what is bad are determined by the people who hand out the rewards and punishments and they are more likely to be based on their own interests, than on the children's interests. It is bad for children to be noisy because their noise disturbs adults. It is good for children to respect their elders because then they do not ask awkward questions.

When the children become adult employees, managers replace parents and teachers. Often what was good as a pupil is bad as an employee, but by the time the child has grown up, he has had enough experience with conflicting definitions of good and bad to accept another set of definitions without great difficulty. So life goes on, with the constant reminder that at the end a completely different set of "goods" and "bads" will be added up and the final reward or punishment will be handed out in the hereafter.

The constant assumption throughout is that someone in a position of authority must decide what is good or bad and someone in authority must hand out rewards and punishments in line with the decision. We have no right to challenge the authority. We may only challenge his fairness in handing out rewards and punishments. This is the basis of all formal grievance procedures.

But suppose we challenge the assumption that someone else must decide what is good or bad for us (or that we must decide what is good or bad for others). If we do that, we gain a new perspective on discipline. We see discipline not as an external value system reinforced or imposed by rewards and punishments, but as an internal understanding reinforced by a subjective or internal reaction to personal actions.

Some 'primitive' peoples, who survive without knowledge of Pavlov's dogs, allow the children to learn the appropriateness of various actions by directly experiencing the effect of their actions. The experience of getting too close to a fire teaches more than a parental reprimand prior to the experience.

I know it is difficult for us to allow our children to experience life. As a boy, I often ran along the tops of railway box cars although it was forbidden by my parents. I never hurt myself doing that, nor did I know any boy who hurt himself that way, but I would still want to prevent my own children from doing it. Similarly, much of what I have learned at work, I have learned through mistakes, but I still want to prevent my staff from making mistakes. But I recognize that as a product of this society. I have been influenced by external authority for good and bad, and by external rewards and punishments. It is possible for me to make an intellectual break but not a complete emotional break, from that influence. Nevertheless, an intellectual break gives a starting point and it should be possible to go beyond that during the transitional stage from authoritarian management to industrial democracy.

In a system of industrial democracy, the goods and the bads (i.e. the work rules) will be defined by the workers themselves. This brings about a fundamental change in the concept of employee discipline which is now related to externally defined goods and bads. As an external authority will not be making the rules, an external authority will not be required to impose the rules by a system of rewards and punishments. The problem of discipline will not be a general problem requiring a general solution, but a specific problem requiring specific solutions applicable to a few people who, for one reason or another, are unable to function effectively in a group.

One of the major difficulties encountered when dealing with serious discipline problems is reconciling the personal needs of the individuals involved with the needs of the other employees in the organization. An employee may not be able to function effectively at work because he is an alcoholic, drug addict or has emotional or psychological problems. Discipline, in the form of punishment, will usually accentuate the personal problem and with our present social system, discipline can be only in the form of punishment. This is not because of malicious managers. Even the most humanitarian managers must accept it as inherent in our social system.

Management texts, which usually make a token bow to humanitarian values, suggest that it is possible for managers to talk over an employee's problems with him without threatening discipline: something along the lines of, "Joe, I think we should have a little chat about a problem you seem to have. Maybe if we talk it over, I will be able to help you."

It's a nice, friendly, non-threatening opener, but if Joe is not a fool, he knows that it means, "Unless you solve your problem, you're fired." It may occasionally help, but more often, the implied threat causes so much worry, the problem becomes worse.

The advantage of this technique is that it allows the manager to believe, when he finally has to fire Joe, that he has done everything he can to help. And he has. The boss-employee relationship combined with a social system that punishes people for having problems, makes it impossible for the manager to arrive at a happy solution.

Perhaps there is no happy solution, but certainly something less unhappy is possible. The boss-employee relationship is often the cause of personal problems that adversely affect work and if the problems have other origins, the relationship makes them worse. Eliminating that relationship, through industrial democracy, eliminates some of the problems and makes solution of others more probable. There will remain, however, the 'hard-core' problems and workers will at times be required to terminate the employment of one of their mates. In so doing, they should not have to toss their mate into a social system which will inflict more punishment on him. The details of such a social system are beyond the scope of this book and are available in other socialist and humanist literature.

Summary

Externally imposed discipline based on externally determined rules, is an integral part of the operations of authoritarian enterprises. With industrial democracy, the rules are determined by the workers concerned and self-discipline replaces external discipline. In exceptional cases where a worker's self discipline is not effective, his co-workers will be required to take corrective action.

chapter fifteen

rules and regulations

WORKING to rule has often been used by employees to slow down work and put pressure on management without going on strike. One of its appeals is that employees can't be reprimanded for carefully following all the company rules as set out in the rule books, regulations or procedures manuals. They are just following orders, but in so doing they can effectively reduce the amount of work done. The more detailed the company rules, the more work will be slowed down by employees who work to rule.

The July 1972 edition of MacLean's Magazine carried an article by former RCMP corporal Jack Ramsey. One of the points made by Mr. Ramsey was that the mass of often petty rules in the RCMP forced the policemen to choose between doing the job expected of officers of the law or following the rules. To do an effective job, rules had to be broken so there was a risk of reprimand just as there was risk of reprimand if the rules were followed and an effective job was not done.

My father, who was for many years a locomotive engineer, maintains that if he had followed all the railway rules he would never have got a train in on time. He retired with an excellent record because he was never responsible for an accident and so was judged by his performance instead of by the rules he broke.

Everyone who has worked on a job which is closely defined by rules and regulations has faced the same kind of thing. A choice has to be made between following the rules or doing the job by shortcuts which bypass the rules. Usually open confrontation is avoided because employees learn that many rules can be ignored with impunity, that others can be broken or bent providing it benefits the employer and that a few rules must always be followed. Managers help employees to recognize the categories by the way they enforce, or do not enforce, the rules, because managers, too, recognize that strict enforcement of all the rules would almost bring work to a stop.

As everyone seems to know that most work rules do more harm than good, it makes one wonder why employees are subjected to more and more of them. I believe that part of the explanation can be found in the fact that corporations operate in a society where there is a prevalent assumption that most people are somewhere between stupid and not very bright — not people like you or me or our friends, of course, but people served by newspapers, magazines, radio, TV, schools and corporations.

Most newspaper and magazine editors work on the assumption about their audiences. Ad writers drop ten years off the assumed mental age. Many teachers work on the assumption that children can learn only if they are trained like animals. Politicians seldom believe that their constituents can safely be fed anything other than pap.

It would be interesting to see what would happen if newspaper and magazine subscribers were able to overhear conversations between freelance writers with something to say and editors who insist that they say it in a watered-down version suitable to their 13-year-old readers. I expect a mass of angry letters and subscription cancellations would follow from readers who became aware of contemptuous attitudes that determine editorial policy.

Key people in the mass media can produce plenty of evidence to support the validity of their assumptions but in doing so they overlook the fact that the evidence is often created by the assumptions. They also overlook the fact that the editors of the only Canadian newspaper that comes close to being a national newspaper assume some intelligence on the part of their readers. Similarly, the TV programs which have aroused the greatest interest were public affairs programs that didn't assume that viewers were stupid. Perhaps that is the reason for political and other pressures terminating those programs. And we can all look back over our school years and recall that the good teachers were those who knew we were capable of learning.

I will not attempt here to influence the editors, producers and teachers who believe in mass stupidity, but I would ask readers to examine their own opinions to make sure that they are not unknowingly influenced by the same belief. For example, does the tendency to slickness in NDP election pamphlets, compared to CCF issue-oriented pamphlets, indicate the influence of the belief in mass stupidity? Does our passive acceptance of infantile advertisements indicate that we think they are appropriate for most people? Does our concurrence in petty, degrading regulations in schools, offices and factories indicate that we feel most people are not bright enough to operate without those regulations?

For industrial democracy to succeed it is important for us to rid ourselves of any latent beliefs in mass stupidity. That is not to say that in certain circumstances the majority of people will not respond to something in a manner that may later appear stupid, but rather that most people are capable of applying much more intelligence than they are usually given credit for. That is not restricted to any kind of intellectual elite. I have many times sat in separate meetings of professors, factory workers, office workers and managers and have detected no difference in the amount of sense applied to the problems they were dealing with. Certainly there are differences in the way problems were approached and discussed, with the professors tending to be concerned with their academic prestige, managers tending to jockey for position, office workers tending to reticence and factory workers tending to direct attack on the problems, but in terms of intelligent solutions, no differences are detectable.

Certainly there is a difference in the results achieved if you ask a group of engineers or a group of lawyers to design a bridge. Technical training and aptitude varies from person to person so you seek help from a mechanic when you have car troubles and help from an accountant when you have tax troubles. The differences in training do not indicate differences in intelligence, and the mechanic's training in no way makes him a judge of whether or not you should be driving a car, nor does the accountant's training make him a judge of whether or not you should move out of Canada to escape Canadian taxes. But we make that kind of assumption when we allow the governing boards of our hospitals and universities to be dominated by businessmen and our parliament to be dominated by lawyers. We consciously and rightly reject it when we select jurors at random from municipal tax rolls.

We must consider the fact that our society and our enterprises require people with differing and highly specialized training. This sometimes leads to the argument that we have no choice but to accept the advice, or orders, and rules and regulations of the experts as we cannot understand as well as they can. This argument is just a device to preserve the status of a privileged elite. Any specialist who says, "We must do such-and-such, but the reasons for it are too complicated to explain to non-specialists", is either a liar or a person who doesn't understand his own specialty. Fortunately, most laymen are now rejecting this elitist argument and, as an example, many people now demand explanations, instead of ex-cathedra pronouncements, from their doctors. When we demand explanations about work rules, we find that many of them can be justified only by the assumption that employees are stupid.

Some rules are required for safety but most other needs for standardization, coordination, quality control and the like, can be better met by concentrating on objectives instead of on rules for achieving those objectives. Concentration on objectives enables the people directly involved in the work to adjust rapidly as they find better ways to meet the objectives, whereas rules written by people not directly involved inhibit progress.

Even safety regulations can often be expressed better in terms of objectives and guidelines rather than rigid rules. One example will illustrate this point.

Recently two families who had cottages close to each other decided to bring electrical power to their cottages. Before connecting the power, the cottages had to be wired and then examined by a Hydro inspector. Wiring in one cabin passed inspection and the other had to be modified to meet Hydro's safety regulations even though the inspector made it clear that it was the safer of the two cabins and, judged in terms of the safety objectives, it was well above Hydro's minimum standards. Unfortunately, it didn't exactly meet the rules and unfortunately someone in Hydro long ago decided that qualified inspectors were not qualified to use common sense. They are not permitted to judge if an installation meets required standards. They may only judge if it meets the rules and regulations. The added cost to the cabin owner is unimportant compared to the cost of the inspector of having to say, "I'm sorry, I know it doesn't make sense, but it's the rule and I have to enforce it." Consider what that does to a person who has to give a similar explanation time after time.

Summary

Enterprises working towards industrial democracy must get rid of all rules and regulations that can be justified only with the assumption of stupidity. In many and perhaps most enterprises, this could best be done by burning all the rules books and starting over again. I make that suggestion seriously, first because it is the most efficient way to tackle the problem and second, because it symbolizes an attitude that is basic to the success of industrial democracy.

chapter sixteen

bigness

IT is fairly simple to calculate the direct financial effect of expanding a business. Usually, if production volumes can be increased, the business can employ more advanced technology which will reduce the unit cost of production. Smaller businesses cannot afford complex automated equipment because the capital cost of such equipment would have to be absorbed by relatively few units of production, whereas larger business can spread the cost over a great many units. This, in simplified form, is the 'economies of scale' argument used to justify big business.

Although it is fairly simple to calculate the direct financial effects of expansion, it is very difficult to calculate the indirect financial and other effects. There is, therefore, a danger of acting on the basis of the simple calculation and ignoring what may be a more important complex calculation.

We have a somewhat schizophrenic attitude towards bigness. We may take pride in helping our community to get bigger, our company to get bigger, or our union to get bigger. Then we complain about the problems of big cities, big companies, and big unions. In fact, we know little about the total effect of bigness and less about managing bigness. It's not that the subject has been overlooked by researchers. Many rising young liberal academics have written papers showing how big institutions alienate people: student dissent in the giant universities, employees of giant corporations who feel like I.B.M. cards, citizens in the giant cities who ignore brutality so long as they themselves are not the objects of the brutality. It is easy to show correlations between bigness and alienation and then conclude that bigness is the cause of alienation. But that is an oversimplification which ignores several other important factors. Let me try to illustrate this with some personal observations.

I have spent a fair bit of time in Montreal, Toronto and Stockholm — three cities of about the same size. I feel less alienated, or more at home, in Stockholm than in Toronto and more at home in Toronto than Montreal. True, this is a personal or subjective feeling but it corresponds to the extent to which the cities are planned with 'me' in mind or were planned with 'they' (businessmen and the rich) in mind. Similarly, I feel more at home when visiting Moscow than New York, although they are both giant cities. I prefer, however, to live in a city much smaller than any of the five mentioned, mainly because when I have free time, I like to get out of the city and into the bush as quickly as possible.

I have been employed by governments and governmental agencies, and small, medium and large privately-owned corporations. The degree of my alienation as an employee was not determined by the size of my employer as much as by whether we did, or did not work, towards a common goal. Much the same thing applies to the relationship between union members and union leaders, regardless of the size of the union.

These personal observations are not intended to dismiss all relationships between bigness and alienation, but rather to indicate that other factors are also involved. Bigness does create problems but it can also solve problems. The difficulty is in knowing when it does which.

The main justification for an enterprise being big is to take advantages of the economies of scale by using advanced technology and specialized manpower. The extent to which economies of scale apply varies greatly from one enterprise to another, and it is impossible to develop a universally applicable formula. We can, however, generalize about some industries providing we recognize that within an industry, there are variations from enterprise to enterprise.

The greatest potential for economies of scale is found in continuous process industries. The potential drops considerably in most manufacturing industries and quickly disappears in most service industries. To illustrate this, giant cement production plants can produce a ton of cement at about one half the cost of its production in smaller and medium size plants, but the difference between the cost of making a car in a smaller or medium size plant or in one of the Detroit giants, is not nearly so great. Turning to the service industries, the cost of accommodating a guest in a large hotel is usually greater than in a small hotel because the economies of scale quickly change to diseconomies.

If we were to carry on with enough examples, the following pattern would emerge:

Characteristics of enterprises with greatest potential for economies of scale

Same product is made for long periods without modification. Available technology enables a high degree of mechanization and automation with realtively few employees. // Quality control is derived from the production process.

Characteristics of enterprises with least potential for economies of scale

Short production and/or frequent product modifications.
Labour intensive
Quality control depends upon people

In enterprises with the greatest potential for economies of scale, it is usually possible to become very large but still retain a form of work organization that enables employees to participate meaningfully in the productive process. This is so because it is fairly easy to identify the connection between specific jobs and the end product of the enterprise. In other enterprises, this relationship may easily be lost in bigness and its loss can be one of the causes of alienation associated with bigness. This can be illustrated by the operation of small and large hotels.

In smaller hotels, all employees are involved in accommodating guests. There will be some division of labour among desk clerks, chambermaids, waiters and chefs, but the work done by each one has an obvious and direct effect on the guests. The guests are people seen by the employees, not just names allocated to room numbers. Similarly, the guests deal with employees who are people.

Most employees in large hotels deal with things, room numbers and voices without bodies. Guests dial various telephone numbers for room service, laundry, complaints, other rooms, local calls, long distance calls and on and on. Voices answer, presumably from the bowels of the hotel, but there is no human contact. Employees' jobs are so fragmented that for many, their work, good or bad, makes no apparent difference to faceless guests.

In an attempt to tie the fragments together into a reasonable operating hotel, rigid work controls are established. To enforce the controls, more supervisors are required. To coordinate the supervisors, more managers are required and so a bureaucracy develops. As in most business bureaucracies, employees and guests become the objects of decisions made by people with whom they have no personal relationship.

This will always happen in service and other labour intensive enterprises unless positive steps are taken to prevent it from happening. The most positive step is to stay small, but that is not always practical even though bigness may lead to higher unit costs. For example, we need large, centrally located hotels in cities, but they do not have to be impersonal, fragmented monstrosities. Any large service enterprise, including a hotel, can be viewed as a coordinated grouping of smaller, self-contained units working in parallel with each other. This concept merits further consideration because it is the key to preventing bigness from leading to alienating conditions.

Most jobs can be divided into a series of sub-tasks which, performed in sequence, complete the job. Thus, when a secretary 'takes a letter' she performs the following tasks:

(1) Goes to the boss's office
(2) Records his dictation in shorthand
(3) Returns to her office
(4) Transcribes her shorthand into a typed letter
(5) Presents the letter to the boss for his signature
(6) If corrections are necessary, repeats 3, 4 and 5
(7) Folds letter, places it in an envelope and mails it

If volume were large enough and we were to apply Taylor's concepts of scientific management, most of these sub-tasks would be handled by a different specialist. If we were to apply Gilbreth's concepts of time and motion study, each specialist would be trained to perform his specialized task without wasted effort or time. If we were to apply common sense, we would know that these fragmented tasks would be meaningless to the persons performing them and a coercive bureaucracy would be needed to force the employees into getting the job done.

While we know this, we often act counter to our knowledge.

We could go to the other extreme of no specialization and have every employee type his own letters and perform every other task required to meet the objectives of the enterprise. Common sense requires the rejection of this extreme along with the other extreme of specialization, but it should be noted that most small enterprises come closer to non-specialization and most large enterprises come closer to complete specialization. It need not be so in most large enterprises which can take advantage of the best of both worlds. This can be illustrated by another look at hotels.

Most large Russian hotels have a very small back-office staff and on each floor they have a woman whom I will call a floor matron. Room telephones are all on direct lines so calls do not go through a hotel switchboard. The services we dial for in our hotels are obtained in Russia through the floor matron. It is as though each floor were a small hotel, both from the point of view of the guest and the matron and other employees working with her. There is no need for the regimentation and paper work needed to tie together the operations of our large hotels. The small groups of employees know what is required to accommodate the guests and they do not need daily written instructions to do their jobs.

Some specialized services are required and it would be impractical to expect every floor matron to provide them all. Guests from many countries may need assistance in their own languages and that kind of specialized service will be centralized in the hotel. But there is a major difference between specializing in a job which allows the specialist to use his full abilities and specializing in a meaningless, fragmented task. By keeping in mind this difference, it is possible to organize work in large service and manufacturing enterprises, in a way which is both economical and humane.

Specialization is justified only when jobs require specialized skills, talent, training or interests. It has no intrinsic justification. When work is organized according to justified specialization, it leads to jobs which have coherence or purpose. To illustrate, the skills and interests of a good secretary, plumber, machinist or accountant are each different and justify specialization. When work is organized on the basis of some theoretical or Taylorist justification for specialization, it leads to fragmented, meaningless tasks.

When only justified specialization is used, a parallel form of job organization evolves naturally. When jobs are fragmented into tasks, a serial form of job organization is required. Using a parallel form of job organization, each employee, or a group of employees working together, carries a job through to a logical conclusion. With a serial form of job organization, each employee performs a repetitive task, and the combination of repetitive tasks by several employees leads to a complete job. In plants, machine shops are typical of parallel organization and assembly lines are typical of serial organization. Offices often have their equivalent of assembly lines, with papers moving from desk to desk and each person contributing his bit to them. Similarly, you can recognize the serial form of job organization in service enterprises when you are shifted from one employee to another before accomplishing some simple thing.

With serial organization, each task performed is dependent upon the task before and the end result is dependent upon the sum of all of the tasks. This dependency makes it vulnerable to bottlenecks and buckpassing. For it to work successfully it requires either a high degree of voluntary cooperation (which is most unlikely), or close supervision which is the first step towards an expensive autocratic hierarchy.

With parallel organization, there is much less interdependency and therefore less vulnerability. The organizational structure does not have to be rigid (as it must be with serial organization) and voluntary cooperation will overcome many problems. This is one of the keys to coping with bigness and it is one of the things which happens naturally when workers themselves determine how their work should be organized.

People involved in big organizations tend to be afraid that the organizations will get out of control unless the members, or employees, are confined in rigid organizational structures and subjected to endless rules and regulations. Control is achieved at the expense of voluntary cooperation which comes through informal human interaction. Replacing that is alienation, not caused by bigness, but caused by the way those in control of big organizations choose to exercise control.

Summary

The theory of economies of scale has a much more limited application than is generally assumed. Many enterprises lose efficiency as they become larger. When economies of scale or other factors demand bigness, alienation can be avoided by a parallel form of organization. This form is likely to emerge as a natural result of industrial democracy.

chapter seventeen

international

IN the following pages I have tried to bring together a description of some practices in other countries that may be useful to Canadians concerned with industrial democracy. I have made no attempt to fully describe the economic organizations in the various countries. Such information is available elsewhere. Nor have I attempted to evaluate the political or economic systems, as my concern is with those things which can be usefully adapted to Canadian conditions or can serve as a warning of what to guard against. My comments are confined to things I have had an opportunity to observe and therefore do not deal with Israel although the kibutsim and Histrudut controlled industries may be significant to a study of industrial democracy.

yugoslavia

It is difficult to write about Yugoslavia without constantly inserting 'on the one hand . . ., but on the other hand . . .'. Yugoslavia is a communist country with no state-owned enterprises. The economic system is highly decentralized with capital flow and prices determined largely by market forces. But there is no private enterprise with the exception of very small shops, each employing not more than 5 people.

The key words are social ownership and self management. Social ownership is a concept distinct from the concept of private or state ownership and implies that neither the state nor private investors can set policies for individual enterprises. Policy-making is the responsibility of the workers.

In each enterprise, an election is held every four years or as otherwise determined by the enterprise, for the position of general manager. The general manager is responsible to a workers council which is elected by the employees every two years. Theoretically, management is accountable to the employees and must operate within the policies established by the employees.

The extent to which the theory and reality of self management coincide varies from one enterprise to another. The formal organizations for self management exist in every enterprise, but in some enterprises genuine worker participation is very limited and in others there is full industrial democracy. In general, self management is more of a reality in the regions which are most economically developed and more of a formality in the least developed regions.

The organizations most influential in shaping the economy of Yugoslavia are the federal and state governments, the communist party, the unions and the workers councils. All of these organizations support the concept of self management both officially and in fact. The same seems true of almost all individual Yugoslavians although the extent of their understanding of the concept varies considerably. In summary, after some 25 years of experience and trial and error with self management, accompanied by progressive decentralization, there is a genuine commitment to the concept.

But does it work?

The answer depends upon the criteria we use to judge success. There are a fair number of people in the major cities who have maids, an apartment in the city, a weekend cottage nearby and a villa on the Adriatic coast. City streets are jammed with small cars driven by people who appear to believe there will be no tomorrow and are determined to prove the accuracy of their belief. Shop windows display all sorts of luxury goods and find customers for them. Clothes are well tailored and of good material. On the giant communal farms with fully integrated production, processing, distribution, housing and holiday facilities, productivity is high and working conditions good.

Then there are the peasants with their small farms worked by horse power, oxen power or woman power, where hours of backbreaking labour produces next to nothing. There are representatives in workers councils who speak about the philosophy of self management and then refer to menial tasks as women's work or to people in another Yugoslavian state as ignorant peasants who don't deserve help from the prosperous regions.

As this is written, there are strong inflationary pressures in Yugoslavia and a serious shortage of hard currency which results not so much from importing western technology as from importing western cars and luxury goods. There are government controls on imports and regulations governing the conditions under which hard currency can be obtained. However, these regulations are regularly bent or circumvented. By way of example, cars cannot usually be imported from the West, but parts for assembly in Yugoslavia can be imported. As a result, Yugoslavia has many auto assembly plants — most of which do little more than put the wheels on cars built elsewhere. The letter of the law, rather than the spirit, is what counts.

This brings us closer to the relevance of the Yugoslavian system to Canada.

Judging by any reasonable standard, Yugoslavia has made great progress in the past 25 years. From a country devastated by war, split many ways by differences in nationalities, languages, alphabets, religions and centuries of hostilities, and containing many illiterate peasants, Yugoslavia has pulled itself into the 1970's, attained near universal literacy and achieved a reasonable standard of living for most people. In the process, it has experimented with self management and reached a higher level of industrial democracy than has been reached in almost any other country in the world.

But there is, in my opinion, a contradiction in the system between the basis of the rewards and the philosophic objectives.

Pay is determined on a points system with each job in an enterprise carrying a certain number of base points. The base points are lowest for manual work and highest for mental work. To the base points are added other points dependent upon the qualifications of the incumbent. The main factors in adding points are the number of years of formal education and the number of years of experience. Finally, the annual distribution of the profit or loss of the enterprise will adjust pay up or theoretically down. Depending upon the nature of the job, the total may often be varied by piece-work or incentive wages.

The effect is a large difference in income between the manual workers in the plant and the specialists in the office. It is difficult to be precise on the disparity because of fringe benefits, including housing supplied by the enterprise, and there are variations from one enterprise to another. However, I did collect a fair bit of data on the subject.

According to official sources the pay disparity from top to bottom within major enterprises is not more than 3 to 1 with some efficient workers actually earning as much or more than those at the top. Semi-official sources said that those at or near the top average five times as much as labourers in the same enterprise.

Unofficial sources placed the ratio at at least 8 to 1 and that is the figure I am inclined to accept as it is supported by obvious major disparities in living standards.

The arguments I listened to in support of piece-rates and major pay disparities could have come from the Canadian Chamber of Commerce, and they are not compatible with the belief that work can be a satisfying, non-alienating experience. Not only are they not compatible with that belief, they work against making that belief a reality. The fact that foremen and managers, other than the general manager, are usually appointed and not elected, aggravates the situation by encouraging an undesirable kind of competition for the rewards of promotion. The same is true with the emphasis on profit which is the measure of success in most enterprises.

There are some differences in the way profit is calculated in Yugoslavia and in Canada and considerable difference in the jargon used to reconcile the concept of profit with the different political ideologies. But the concept itself is the same in both countries and its use as a measure of success and rewards (particularly for managers) has all of the dangers discussed in a previous chapter. Even the attempts to exert some discipline through the Party representatives in enterprises does not change the fact that having established profit as a major criterion of management success, management behaviour will reflect that criterion. Of course, social ownership and the ultimate power of the workers councils reduces abuse and exploitation of the workers for the sake of increasing profit, but it does not prevent the clouds of smoke from factory chimneys drifting over Zagreb. Nor does it prevent the constant circumvention of socially and economically desirable laws. In fact, it places a premium on those who have the ability to bend laws in favour of enterprise profit just as it rewards those who achieve gain for the enterprise at the expense of the community.

The exceptions are the agricultural communes. Because of their importance it is worth describing one of the larger communes known as PKB.

PKB has over 200,000 acres of productive land and about 17,000 employees. Its operations are spread over much of Yugoslavia but the largest single unit is located a few miles from Belgrade, whose population of about 1 million is very dependent upon PKB for food. The commune produces, processes and markets a full range of agricultural products including meat, dairy products, fruit, vegetables, preserves and wine, as well as by-products such as glue. It has a major research centre and a number of holiday resorts for members and tourists. Employees (or members) and their families live in small, attractive towns on the commune. There is no distinction and therefore no conflict, between the immediate communities and the enterprise as they are all part of the same self-managed commune.

PKB has over 300 work units, each consisting of a group of people doing similar work at one location. Each unit has a foreman and a miniature workers council.

Related work units are coordinated by sixty-four departments, each with a manager and workers council. The departments are coordinated by eight divisions similarly organized. Finally, there is the general manager and the main workers council which sets overall policy.

At the time I visited PKB some changes in the constitution were being considered. These were being discussed in the work units and their recommendations were being fed to the main body of the workers council. In addition, views were exchanged through the commune's weekly newspaper. My impression was that there was genuine widespread participation and that the outcome would reflect the views of the members.

Viewed as a self-contained community, PKB could be described as a social and economic success. From the country's point of view it is also a success as it is far more efficient than the small private farms. But in considering this broader viewpoint, I recall my interpreter asking a PKB representative why there was a meat shortage in Belgrade that week. The reply was: "That's simple to explain. We have approval for a price increase next week and we are holding back supplies until then."

If you make profit the god, you must expect sacrifices to be made to him.

There is much we can learn from Yugoslavian experience. On the negative side, we can see the problems created by the contradiction between ideological objectives and the criteria for measuring success of individuals and enterprises. On the positive side, we have proof that industrial democracy can work even when the odds are much more against it than they are in Canada where we have a firmer economic and educational base on which to build.

Yugoslavia is a very loose federation of states held together in part by great and widespread respect for President Tito. On the assumption that Yugoslavia will survive as an independent country in the post-Tito era, I would like to speculate on the future for its system of self management.

There are two major forces working against each other — the commitment to self-management in a socialist society and the commitment to techniques that encourage a capitalist value system. Yugoslavian economists with whom I discussed this conflict tended to ignore it on the grounds that it wasn't an economic problem. Trade union leaders and political representatives tended to rationalize away the conflict with some intriguing interpretations of Marx. Young people seemed the most concerned about conflict.

The reliance on profits and large wage disparities to provide incentive is partly a reaction to the Soviet Union and partly a belief that they represent the shortest route to economic growth. It is assumed that social ownership will prevent the abuse which comes when these techniques are used in capitalist economies. Unfortunately, when people are asked to cooperate like socialists but are rewarded for competing like capitalists, the rewards are going to influence behaviour and a continuation of this could transform Yugoslavian self-management from an active process to a formalized ritual. My guess, however, is that the process is now so deeply rooted that it will be the dominant one of the two conflicting forces. If so, the economic techniques will be brought in line with the philosophical beliefs and the development of industrial democracy will continue.

west germany

Every country is, to some extent, a captive of its history and Germany is that to a greater extent than most. One speaks of pre-1933 or post-1945 Germany, leaving a gap for the fascist aberration. But the gap is significant for socialists and trade unionists who remember it and it goes a long way towards explaining their current emphasis on political and economic stability.

Many international surveys of industrial democracy include details of the German system of co-management. It is too important to be ignored, but it is questionable if it is, in fact, a form of industrial democracy.

Co-management refers to equal labour-capital representation on the supervisory board (roughly, the board of directors) of privately owned enterprises. It was a pre-1933 union demand, but was not put into practice until 1951. The 1951 co-management law applies only to coal mining and the iron and steel industry and was more the result of Allied pressure to prevent a rebuilding of the Krupp munitions cartel than of any desire on the part of the new German capitalist government.

The supervisory boards establish broad corporate policy and select the management board which is responsible for day-to-day operations. The industrial relations or personnel manager can be selected and removed only with the approval of the labour representatives on the supervisory board so he is, in effect, the labour nominee on the management board.

Before going into more detail, let me quote two passages from *Codetermination rights of the workers in Germany,* published in English in 1967 by the DGB (German Trade Union Federation).

Such a general conception of co-determination presupposes a system of free enterprise based on the principle of a free market economy. In all those instances in which the economy is subjected to a central administration there can therefore be no genuine form of workers' co-operation or co-determination at the various levels of the productive process. All really important decisions affecting the volume and type of production, as well as the forms of administration within the economic system, are made by the central authorities and the ministries, with the result that there is little or no room left for co-determination and joint responsibility at enterprise and workshop level. Any form of co-determination to be exercised inside the undertakings by those affected by the processes of the economy, and particularly by the workers, is practically ruled out.

Co-determination places no restrictions on the legitimate rights of the owners of the means of production. But rights of property justify at best a control over things, never a control over men. It is unworthy of a free order of society that some men, merely because they own the means of production, should exercise mastery over other men.

The "free enterprise socialism" indicated by these quotations is in line with many conversations I had in 1972 with German trade unionists and members of the Social Democratic Party. They differed from my conversations with representatives of capitalism only in reference to what the relative powers of capital and labour should be.

As this is being written, there is a heated debate in Germany concerning the extension of the parity co-management laws to all large enterprises. The Social Democratic Party and the DGB are pushing for equal labour-capital representation on the supervisory boards, whereas the Christian Democratic Party (CDU) and industrialists are holding to a formula that would have the supervisory boards made up of representatives of labour, management and capital — thus assuring the workers of a minority position. It appears likely that the Free Democrats, who hold the balance of power, will force some compromise settlement.

It might appear that here would be a conflict in union roles if the union were negotiating with an enterprise where half the supervisory board members were union representatives. In fact, the problem doesn't arise because bargaining is industry-wide and takes place between representatives of the DGB and the Employers' Federation.

Co-management has some relevance to economic democracy and the balancing of powers of vested interests, but it has little connection with industrial democracy. Although the extension of co-management is the cause of heated political debate in Germany, public opinion polls have indicated that it ranks very low in the minds of most workers.

This is to be expected as the union representatives tend to assume the values of the capitalist representatives and like them go to and from work in chauffeur-driven Mercedes. Also, co-determination has little relevance to the shop floor.

Of more relevance to industrial democracy is the legislation passed in late 1971 which extends the rights of works councils.

The first elections for works council representatives were held in the spring of 1972 and there hasn't yet been time to evaluate the effect of the new legislation on working conditions. I am, however, not optimistic and would be reluctant to use the German experiment as a model for Canada even though it provides for a degree of shop-floor democracy on a consultation basis. Like much German legislation related to work, it is influenced by a desire to define the rights of various groups rather than eliminating the barriers between the groups.

One should not overlook the fact that Germany has had virtually full employment for several years so most workers can change jobs if their bosses are unreasonable or the working conditions poor. That reality may have more influence on industrial democracy than all the legislation.

sweden

When a country's gross national product is divided by its population, some tiny oil sheikdoms (and the U.S.A.) show a very high standard of living. When we start our calculations with the reality for the majority of the people in a country, the Swedes enjoy the world's highest standard of living. No other country has gone so far in eliminating problems of poverty, unemployment, health, education, housing and disabilities. And no other country is so aware of the problems still ahead on the road towards socialism.

Interest in industrial democracy in Sweden is best seen in the light of current interest in equality — a subject much researched in recent years and well summarized in *Towards Equality: The Alva Myrdal Report to the Swedish Social Democratic Party,* published in English by the Party in 1971. The following quotations are from a section called 'What do we mean by equality?'

> *Human and social relationships.* Greater equality in conditions of living is not merely a goal in itself. Great disparities in standards and influence complicate and poison relationships and communication between individuals and groups. Socialism should be seen as a freedom movement, in which freedom from the pressure of external circumstances, class divisions and insecurity is considered a *prerequisite* for new human relationships marked more by cooperation and community and less by self-assertion, competition and conflict among various groups in society. Equalizing conditions of life then become a means of changing human relationships, of creating a better social climate. The co-operation which the Social Democrats aim at should take place on equal terms and between equals.
>
> *An efficient society.* The traditional middle-class criticism of the equality policy of the Social Democratic Party is that greater equality must be

bought at the price of reduced efficiency, slower economic growth, etc.
It may be replied, however, that even in terms of efficiency it is gross
mismanagement to allow only the better-situated to develop their inherent
talents and fully express themselves in society. Groups which are lagging
behind, with unused resources to contribute to the common good, are
a hindrance both to efficiency and to desirable social change.

We are thinking not only of equality in the *utilization* of all of society's
facilities and resources. The concept of equality concerns just as much
the possibility of *influencing* the choice of what goods, services, cultural
experiences, environmental qualities will be available in society.

This applies to:

Economic democracy on the parliamentary level; that is to say, the
citizens' right to express themselves as voters on guidelines for production and economic life in general, and consequently about future consumption possibilities and environmental conditions. The disputes of the
fifties and the sixties in Sweden regarding the public sector should be
considered in this context.

Democratic conditions at the grassroot level, that is to say, the opportunity for the individual, in cooperation with others, to influence his
own immediate life situation, in working life, in schools and institutions
in his living environment.

The Social Democrats' view of equality means that, where Nature has
created great and fundamental differences in abilities, these must *not* be
allowed to determine the individual's chances in life, but rather that
society should intervene to "restore the balance". These differences,
in the form of physical or intellectual handicaps, can never be eliminated,
but they can be reduced in a generous social climate, and one can work
against their leading to social discrimination. Disadvantages inflicted by
Nature should not be accepted as something we can do nothing about.

This concept of equality goes far beyond the equalization of incomes. That is not far from a reality now. Except for the lower five
per cent and upper five per cent in the economic strata, the remaining
ninety per cent have incomes ranging from about 2,000 to 5,000
crowns a month. But with a progressive income tax, housing subsidies
and a variety of transfer payments, the actual disposable income varies
by only about five hundred crowns or $100 a month.

In addition to the efforts to create a more egalitarian society, the
following factors have an important bearing on the progress towards
industrial democracy in Sweden:

A Social Democratic government (or coalition) for the past 40 years
A powerful trade union movement
Virtually full employment
High standard of education
Comprehensive welfare programs

The 'rights' of capital are curtailed by the State and the unions
much more than in Canada. Shareholders, through their managers,
cannot unilaterally decide to close a plant, make major technological
changes or in general, exercise the whims known in Canada as management prerogatives. It is against this background that current developments in Sweden can be understood.

Capital and labour are cooperating in a series of experiments
in various aspects of industrial democracy.

These are carefully controlled experiments and 'before and after' results will be carefully analyzed. So far, very little concrete information about results has been published although I received some glowing reports about these experiments. The cooperation between capital and labour may seem strange and it is sometimes attributed to the progressive attitude of Swedish capitalists. It should be noted, however, that capitalists always appear progressive when there is no alternative to dealing with a strong union movement backed by a socialist government.

Besides the controlled cooperative experiments, there are numerous other enterprises with varying degrees of workers participation or industrial democracy. In the state owned Kiruna iron mines north of the Arctic circle, there is a large measure of control over work by the workers brought about, in part, by government policy, in part, by a wild-cat strike. In Gotenburg, Volvo has replaced assembly lines by work crews responsible for producing complete components and having some degree of self management. This change has been well publicized as an example of how progressive management increased productivity and job satisfaction. Less well publicized is the fact that Volvo had no choice but to make the change. Few workers were prepared to stay on assembly lines when alternative employment was readily available.

Sweden has seldom relied upon legislation to control labour-management relations nor are the Swedes legislating industrial democracy. They are, instead, consolidating gains and creating conditions for further developments. Accompanying this is a continual movement towards economic democracy as functional socialism gradually transfers power at the top from capitalists to the people. This process will probably speed up as the huge pension fund becomes the major source of capital.

As my concern in this book is to chart a course towards industrial democracy in Canada, there is no need to go into details of Swedish techniques that cannot be transplanted to Canada. What can be transplanted is the concept of parallel movements towards economic democracy (democratic control over major economic decisions) and towards industrial democracy (democratic control of working life). Neither can succeed without the other.

An interesting project to democratize the Swedish civil service is underway. This merits some attention as it has direct relevance to Canada. When the decision was made recently to enable civil servants to control their work lives democratically, certain technical problems were immediately apparent. A distinction had to be preserved between policy and operational decisions. Policy is the responsibility of the Riksdag (parliament) and could not be delegated to civil servants who are responsible for operating in accordance with government policy. Under Swedish law, the general director of each ministry (roughly equivalent to the deputy minister of a government department in Canada) assumes ultimate responsibility for the operations of his department. As could be expected, the people who accepted ultimate responsibility wished also to have ultimate control. This, however, would prevent true democracy from developing in the departments.

As usual the Swedes decided to establish the conditions necessary for democracy and then allow the democratic process to develop at its own pace. The pace has varied greatly amongst the departments.

A central committee was established to provide guidance during the transition. Each department was approached with the suggestion that a decision committee be established. Most departments established a decision committee chaired by the general director and having equal labour and management representation — usually 4 or 5 representatives from each side. Ultimate responsibility, formerly vested in the general directors, was transferred to the committees.

Shortly after the project began, the Government made a decision to decentralize some operations. The decision would lead to the transfer of about 6,000 civil servants from Stockholm to smaller cities or towns. All hell broke loose with the civil servants maintaining that democracy in work was a farce if they couldn't decide where they were going to work. This was the first major test of the distinction between policy and operational decisions. Decentralization was government policy and even though it had a major impact on the 6,000 civil servants, parliamentary democracy had to take precedence over work democracy. However, the implementation of the policy requires new facilities in various cities and towns. The operational decisions concerning site locations, building designs, office layouts and work organization are being made democratically by the workers directly involved.

Earlier in this chapter I suggested that the high standard of education was a factor in the development of industrial democracy in Sweden. The high standard does not refer to the amount of information acquired in school (although that is impressive) but to the fact that the educational system encourages the pupils to cooperate as a group with the stronger helping the weaker. Personal achievement is encouraged but not at someone else's expense. For Karl to do better, Erik does not have to do worse. For Karl to win, Erik does not have to lose. In school, children learn to participate in making decisions and they learn, through experience, to accept the responsibility that goes with authority.

Conservatives criticize the schools on the grounds that they are instruments of socialist propaganda. And they are. Just as our schools are instruments for capitalist propaganda. It is impossible for schools to be neutral in the values they impart even if politics are never mentioned. I anticipate that some readers will object to my references to Sweden as a socialist country. Their objection has some validity when Sweden is measured against traditional definitions of socialism. I am, however, not overly concerned about the semantics. I have been in countries where the formal structures of socialism were more developed but none where the essence of socialist life was so advanced.

norway

If we think about Norway at all, we probably think about a country of mountains, lakes, rivers and fjords, populated by sailors, skiers and Thor Heyerdal riding his Kontiki raft. Hardly the picture of a country in the process of making industrial democracy a reality.

But let's add to the picture. Norway is indeed a country of mountains and water and it has the world's fourth largest merchant navy. But except for officers, you will find few Norwegians on Norwegian ships. They are manned by crews from countries not enjoying Norway's full employment and affluence. And between ski trips, the Norwegians have created a strong labour union movement (going back more than a century). The union — LO — has been a major factor in electing a labour government which has held power with a few interruptions, for nearly forty years. The Norwegian police may have set a world record that can be checked by readers concerned by such things. They haven't shot a union organizer in this century.

Once again I hesitate to say, "They did it and so can we". Norway is not Canada. It has a population of just under four million people with a common history, language, culture and religion. The labour union strength has led to a long period of labour-management cooperation unparalleled in Canada. The German occupation during World War II did much to break class barriers and unite Norwegians against a common enemy. So conditions favoured an extension of democracy into working life. One of those conditions is respect for workers because they are people, which is very different from respect for workers because they are necessary to the production process.

The trade union federation — LO — bargains country wide with the employers federation — NAF — every two years. They update the Basic Agreement which, with the exception of the war years, has been in effect since 1935. The Basic Agreement establishes the labour-management relationship in most enterprises and forms the first part of almost all collective agreements between Norwegian employers and employees. Although not all employees are members of the LO, nor all employers members of the NAF, the strength of these organizations is such that they establish the pattern for the whole country.

The Basic Agreement recognizes the right of employees, through their shop stewards, to be consulted on most issues directly affecting the workers. As will be discussed later, actual practice often goes well beyond consultation to joint control or workers' decisions.

Legislation passed by the Labour government in 1972 and effective in January 1973, provides for direct workers representation on the policy making and management boards of most enterprises. Unlike the German co-management laws which enable outside trade unionists to serve on some boards of directors, the Norwegian legislation provides that the representatives must be employees of the enterprise. The legislation is vague and will require clarification through regulations, but generally speaking it provides for employees to have one third representation at the top decision making levels. This can be considered as a first step supplementing shop floor democracy provided by the Basic Agreement. If the trend indicated by amendments to the Basic Agreement is projected a few years ahead and coupled with the new legislation, it is reasonable to predict considerable industrial democracy in the not-too-distant future.

Like Sweden, Norway has a LO-NAF Cooperation Council concerned with advancing labour participation in work. The Norwegian Council, however, goes beyond its Swedish counterpart in that its full-time secretariat is dedicated to ending worker alienation even though that could lead to an end to the traditional privileges of capital and management. I do not intend to suggest that capitalists are doing so with great enthusiasm but rather that the logic of circumstances is such that no other direction is reasonable.

Two companies will serve to illustrate developments in Norway and, more important, provide ideas for Canada. The first, producing made-to-order heavy equipment, is typical of Norwegian companies in that it is fairly small (about 350 employees) and most of the workers are highly skilled (in this case, machinists). It is also typical in terms of the degree of worker participation.

My initial impression of the enterprise was that the management was simply consulting workers on matters directly affecting them, as required by the Basic Agreement. Later, I realized that almost all important matters were discussed with workers committees and although management were not bound by the workers recommendations, their influence was so great that they certainly were not easily ignored. Foremen in theory had the traditional powers of crew bosses but in fact are closer to coordinators. In discussion with the personnel manager, I asked whether there were many grievances and on being told that there weren't many, I pushed for specific figures. The reply I received was, "I have been with the company for 2 years and there has only been one grievance during that time."

The grievance was filed about two weeks before my visit and it was a charge by a worker that his foremen frequently acted in an authoritarian manner. The personnel manager and plant engineer spoke to the foreman, who was respected for his technical ability, and tried to explain that he must obtain the cooperation of his workers and not give orders. They were not optimistic about the chances of the foreman changing his attitude so the grievance would be resolved by replacing the foreman by someone acceptable to the workers.

Two main factors seemed to be responsible for management's willingness to go beyond the terms of the Basic Agreement. One was a desire to try to make work satisfying because it was the right thing to do.

The other was an awareness that any one of the skilled workers could easily find employment elsewhere.

The second example is Norsk Hydro, located near Porsgrunn in southeast Norway. Far from being typical, Norsk Hydro is one of Norway's largest enterprises with 5,000 employees at the Porsgrunn plants. It is a continuous process industry operating 24 hours a day, seven days a week. Its main products are fertilizer, magnesium and other chemical compounds. The Norwegian government owns fifty-one per cent of the shares and the remaining private shareholders are disbursed in a number of countries.

In 1967, a decision was made to experiment with workers' participation in one of the fertilizer plants. This would appear to be a strange choice as the highly mechanized process seemed to offer little opportunity for judgment or participation by workers. The technology appeared to dictate machine control rather than workers control. It is for this reason that I have included Norsk Hydro as an illustration of what can be done under adverse circumstances.

Prior to 1967, the company had a typical hierarchical organization and workers performed their allotted tasks in their allotted locations in the plants. In 1967 an action committee was established in the fertilizer plant. The committee began with six members representing management and the union. It was given a free hand with the understanding that decisions made on matters such as wage systems and work organization should have no immediate consequences outside the experimental area.

The experiment fell into three phases:

(1) An introductory or information phase with steady contact between the committee and employees.
(2) A decision phase during which employees were able to be directly involved in the project.
(3) An action phase during which ideas were implemented.

The implementation of ideas led to several major changes summarized for me by the Chief Engineer, Mr. Olav Haug, as follows:

"A new organization gradually emerged and has continued to emerge in the department. Methods changed from individual to work group. The workers have found it convenient to help each other and to learn from each other.

Different patterns of job rotation have been worked out allowing the workers to extend their knowledge and reduce the monotony of their job.

This also has resulted in important changes for the foremen, the superintendent and also the engineers, both in staff and line. They can now concentrate more steadily on boundary control and regulation.

The interest for learning both jobs and more fundamental knowledge has been awakened among a great part of the workers. Shift operators have shown interest in learning mechanical and instrumental work, and workers from the mechanical group have demonstrated interest in possessing knowledge and better insight into their ordinary profession.

A new paying system has been developed, paying people for what they can do, (i.e. the number of jobs they have learned) and not as in earlier systems for what they do. In addition we have ended up with a bonus system based on criteria which the employees themselves can influence: quantity, costs, loss of materials and working hours.

As a summary I may dare say: The organization activity started up in 1967 has demonstrated that most of the collaborators are interested in finding better solutions of the activities within an industrial organization like ours. The workers represent knowledge and resources which can be turned to account. It is up to the leaders of the groups of parties to agree on working together instead of working against each other."

Mr. Haug's comments tend to understate the changes. To eliminate classes of workers, floor cleaners were absorbed into the regular work force, the workers now clean their work areas in their spare time. Foremen became coordinators instead of bosses. One foreman died a year before my visit and hadn't been replaced at the time of my visit. The work crew were sharing the responsibilities for coordination. The control centre for the factory was opened to employees and the mystery removed from the graphs and flashing lights that signal the inner workings of the complex machinery. In fact, the control room has become just one more work place which employees can rotate through.

A year after the experiment began, it moved out of the experimental stage and a policy of workers' participation became applicable to all of Norsk Hydro's operations near Porsgrunn.

The traditional chain of command and lines of communication have been eliminated and employees seek help or advice from anyone likely to be able to provide it.

The transition was not always easy. Not all managers could adjust to a new philosophy of work based on respect for the dignity of workers. Several managers had to be dismissed because their presence would be harmful to the objectives.

Presumably there are still actions that are unacceptable, but I was unable to determine what process is used for discipline. The response of the workers, when questioned about this was, "We take care of our problems". In the few extreme cases when management action is required, the solution is usually agreed upon by the workers before management becomes aware of the problem.

I am optimistic about the future for industrial democracy in Norway. Shop-floor democracy is already quite widespread. The new legislation providing workers' representation in the key decision-making boards will introduce another element of industrial democracy. Finally, and most important, enough people are prepared to reject the traditional management concepts that conflict with their belief in human dignity.

chapter eighteen

economics

A full-scale discussion of economics is beyond the scope of this book but some misconceptions promulgated by journalists, politicians and others, must be corrected in order for industrial democracy to be acceptable.

Despite the smokescreen put up by economists who frequent TV panel shows, our economic system is not a mystery capable of penetration only by a chosen few. The study of economics is the study of the effects of allocating scarce resources. We have unlimited wants but limited resources to meet those wants. We lose track of this fact in Canada because we have got used to having unused human and material resources; but imagine the situation if every person who wished to work were fully employed. Then imagine that we wanted 100 new hospitals. To build them we must not only allocate manpower and materials to their construction, we must deny the manpower and materials to other building projects. By learning or acquiring more efficient ways of doing things we are able to satisfy more of our wants with the resources available. By leaving some of our resources idle, (e.g. through unemployment) we are able to satisfy fewer of our wants.

Who, then, decides how resources in the form of manpower, material and equipment will be allocated amongst all of our wants? The free enterprise answer is that market forces or the law of supply and demand determine their allocation. Actually, federal, provincial and municipal governments and a large number of public boards and agencies are the main bodies in deciding resource allocation. Next in importance are the large corporations which are not subject to the market forces, but control them through advertising and by dominating both the sources of supply and the distribution outlets. A long way behind, consumer preferences have a slight influence on resource allocations.

The people who decide on the allocation of resources also decide on prices. Prices are not determined by an invisible hand or by any laws of economics. Businessmen set the prices of the goods and services they sell. Governments and their agencies set prices for their services. There is no necessary connection between the cost and the selling price. We pay directly to cover the cost of a few government services but most are covered indirectly by taxation. The same is true of the goods and services offered by large corporations. They do not charge customers directly for the massive advertising campaigns, empire-building in executive suites or their image-building efforts. These costs are covered indirectly through higher selling prices which, in effect, are taxation of customers by corporations. Not only is this taxation without representation, it is taxation most often determined in the board rooms of foreign countries.

The Trudeau government insistence in the late 1960's and early 1970's that we needed high unemployment to control inflation mystified most non-economists. Somehow, it just didn't tally with common sense and it did so even less when we got both high unemployment and inflation. It appeared that Trudeau and his economic advisors were incompetent, when they were actually being less than honest by not revealing that the government chooses to conduct the economic battle with both hands tied behind its back.

There are a number of international factors which tend to increase costs in Canada and they are largely beyond our control. The American war in Indo-China has been one of those factors and growing worldwide demands for natural resources have been another. These inflationary pressures do not worry the large corporations because they can recover the extra costs and use them as an argument for unwarranted price increases and larger profits. Forcing several hundred thousand Canadians out of work was not going to change that situation and Trudeau's advisors knew it. But they also knew that full employment would greatly strengthen organized labour's bargaining position and so restrict industrialists from acting only in their own interest. Industrialists do not finance the Liberal Party to encourage it to be kind to unions.

Far from controlling inflation, unemployment adds to inflation because people who are unemployed must live and that costs something for which we get no production in return. There is no economic reason for unemployment in Canada. The reasons are political. In most of West Europe the existence or threat of a socialist government makes full employment a political necessity. So there is full employment in most of West Europe and economists be damned.

Let us turn to money, those pieces of paper we carry in our wallets. That's just what they are — pieces of paper, but they are pieces of paper with a special significance to our lives and economy, and they have been endowed with a mystique. Stripped of the mystique, money is just a means of simplifying the exchange of goods and services. It is a ruler for measuring the price of things relative to other things and it has no value in itself. It acquires value only because we accept it as a standard of measurement knowing that we can pass it along to others who will accept it in the same way. If faith in its acceptability is lost, it loses its value. That often happens in countries defeated in war and when it does, some new exchange medium evolves. For a short time after the Second World War the exchange medium in Germany (that is, the money) was cigarettes.

As Canada is a major trading nation, the value of our dollars in relation to the currencies in other countries is of considerable interest to us. Despite the endless articles on the subject as we move from one international monetary crisis to another, there is very little understanding of the subject. This is partly because there is an apparent paradox which is seldom explained. If our economy is healthy at home we encounter foreign exchange troubles. If our economy is sluggish, we overcome these troubles. This happens because a healthy growing economy with full employment increases confidence in our money and increases its value in relation to foreign currencies. At the same time, the healthy economy puts more money into circulation so more is available for imports. Our increased supply of money at a higher international value then buys more goods in other countries and their money buys less in our country, so it becomes easier to import and harder to export. Businesses move away from Canadian-made goods towards foreign-made goods and the economy weakens. The weakening of the economy reduces the international value of our money and we start the cycle all over again. There are rules governing this game which is played by most western industrialized countries, but every one of the countries breaks the rules regularly.

There is no need for this ridiculous situation to carry on indefinitely. It was created by people and can be changed by people by setting exchange rates through the world bank in a manner that eliminates exchange speculation.

Capital is a much misunderstood word and deserves some space in this diversion into economic mythology. Let us suppose that we are part of a group of people who have decided to establish an independent community in a remote wilderness area. The area in which we settle has much fertile land but is now covered with trees. Water and natural resources are plentiful. Summers are warm and sunny and winters cold and snowy. We arrive in the spring with our clothes, enough food to last for two months, some axes and hand tools, a few horses and our human abilities.

The need to survive determines what we may do. Land must be cleared so we can grow food and shelters must be built before winter. For some time all our efforts are directed towards survival but eventually we get a little ahead and are able to store up more than enough food to get us through the next winter, to spend time making more and better tools and plows and to improve our houses. In economic parlance, our capital (the things we have produced and not used up) has increased. A closer look shows that we have three different kinds of capital — food to sustain us, houses to live in and tools and plows that will make us more productive in the future. We now have some choice in how we plan our economic future as our actions are no longer completely determined by the need to survive. With an eye to the future rather than immediate comforts, we realize that if our capital included a few tractors we would be much more productive but to make tractors we would have to have the know-how to mine and process metals and fabricate the metals into workable machines. It could be done but it would take many years and leave us with almost no time to make our shelters and clothing more comfortable; that is, we would have to give up some immediate improvements in our standard of living in order to get a greater improvement some years later. Alternatively, we can try to get tractors from a community which has some to spare; that is we can try to take advantage of foreign capital to accelerate our long-term development without sacrificing our current standard of living.

Unless we are recognized as an underdeveloped country eligible for foreign aid, we will get foreign capital (in this case, tractors) only if we are able to offer in return something the foreigners want. We may have surplus food which they are willing to accept in exchange for tractors, in which case the transaction is concluded and presumably everyone goes home happy. Or we may not have anything to exchange now but we believe that if we had the tractors for five years we could produce a kind of vegetable much desired in the foreign country. One tractor now has a relative value of 1000 bushels of the vegetables, but we may agree to get the tractors now and pay 1200 bushels for each one at the end of five years, because we believe the extra cost (interest) is worthwhile. Alternatively, we may decide not to borrow capital and pay interest on it, so instead we say to the foreigners, "We have a fertile land with great resources. Bring your tractors and knowhow in and we will help you exploit our resources by working for your companies." Canada is one of a very few countries to have made that choice without being threatened by military force.

Moving into the present, the nature of capital has not changed although the variety and complexity of capital goods has increased. We tend to confuse real capital with the pieces of paper that facilitate its exchange — money, bonds, shares and various credit systems. When the shares of a Canadian corporation are bought by foreigners, we do not add to our capital but only change its control. If foreigners provide us with more advanced technology, it increases our real capital and leaves us with the decision of what to offer in return.

With some of the mythology out of the way, let us consider what is or is not economically possible:

> We can have full employment by which I mean that every person who wishes, can have an opportunity to work or an opportunity to receive training and other assistance that will enable him to work.
> We can prevent business and industry from exploiting a healthy economy with unjustified price increases.
> We can cut housing costs by eliminating land speculation and reducing interest rates and the cost of many other essentials can be cut by a rational transportation program.

It is political expediency, not economics, that prevents us from doing these things.

We cannot, however, prevent a number of international factors from increasing some of our costs and ultimately prices. This is nothing to worry about providing:

> (1) Some groups of people, such as old age pensioners, are not left behind.
> (2) The rate of price increases is in line with increases in other industrialized countries.

Now back to the basic economic question — our unlimited wants and our limited resources to meet those wants. We must choose amongst the wants. We cannot, for example, overnight replace the slums in Canada and throughout the world with good housing and we cannot suddenly assure everyone of adequate food. What we set as our priorities is determined by our personal values and not by economics. Those who say that the choices must be made according to market forces or the law of supply and demand, are just expressing their belief that when there is not enough for everyone, allocation (or rationing) *should* be determined by ability to pay. If you change the value system, you can change bases of allocation as we have already done, for example, with medical care and hospitalization. Besides changing the way we allocate goods and services, we can meet more of our wants by making better use of our resources. Industrial democracy will make better use of our resources and, I believe, it will lead to a shift in emphasis from the artificially created wants for prestige symbols, towards the needs that must be met so that people can live in dignity.

Summary

What is, or is not, economically feasible depends primarily on our ability and willingness to mobilize and allocate our economic resources. Many economists who try to explain why this or that cannot be done, are just using economic jargon to rationalize their conservative tendencies.

Instead of allowing dubious economic theory to govern our economic and social development, we should start with our values and goals, then seek the economic means to achieve them.

chapter nineteen

ownership

S OONER or later, discussions on industrial democracy get hung up on questions of ownership of enterprises and the conflict between owners, as represented by managers and workers. As soon as one advocates this much or that much public or private ownership, one is placed on the left, right or centre of the political spectrum. Without wishing to avoid taking a stand, I would prefer to approach the question from a point of view more relevant to industrial democracy.

When we say we own something, we may be referring to owner-ship as recognized in law and also ownership as a gut feeling. I don't pretend to understand the gut feeling of ownership but I have been suf-ficient evidence of its existence and effects to believe it is a factor which must be considered in order to grasp the concept of ownership.

Several years ago, while visiting the U.S., I came to know two young Texans. Both were university graduates, apparently of normal intelligence, and both owned property in Texas. One of them made a reference to shooting at any stranger who trespassed on his property and the other agreed that that was the proper thing to do. When I indicated that I thought this was somewhat extreme I was told, "But it's my property." No other justification seemed necessary to him. Obviously, he had a feeling of ownership which I couldn't share, so we were arguing on different planes.

Galsworthy, in the *Man of Property* refers to the Forsytes' highly developed sense of property. That gut feeling of ownership was well portrayed in the T.V. serial, The Forsyte Saga.

Owner-managers of businesses sometimes close their businesses permanently rather than recognize a trade union. They are reacting to the gut feeling of ownership.

The gut feeling seems to say, "This is mine to do with as I please. Anything I choose to do with it is legitimate, good and right. Anything that restricts my choice is wrong. Anything I do to prevent others from using what is mine is justified because I have absolute rights over what I own." It should be noted that this is very different from the feeling of being part of one's environment and enjoying nature's beauty. That is a feeling of harmony, whereas the gut feeling of ownership is antagonistic.

The legal rights associated with ownership are quite different and vary with what is owned. Ownership of your toothbrush gives you exclusive rights of use and disposal. Car ownership does not carry the same rights. Your car may be commandeered by police for emergency use and the way you use it is circumscribed by many laws. In some provinces, there is control over disposal as well.

Home ownership (the one with the real gut feeling) does not carry with it exclusive or unconditional rights. Police, firemen and various inspectors may, under certain conditions, enter your home. You cannot destroy your home or add to it without permission from local governments. In fact, your rights associated with home ownership do not extend much beyond choosing colour schemes, making minor modifications, having some privacy and selling it if you can find a buyer. As tenants gain more rights, their position becomes very similar to home owners, except for the gut feeling.

Corporate ownership used to carry rights comparable to toothbrush ownership, but with much more serious implications. Not too long ago it was accepted that owners of corporations were free to expand, contract and close down, discriminate in hiring and firing and generally do as they pleased because "It's my company". Political expediency and trade union pressure have curtailed the rights of owners of corporations. Federal or provincial laws regulate maximum working hours and minimum pay rates, forbid discrimination in employment and price fixing, require maintenance of financial records and independent audits. Municipal zoning influences building locations and constructions. Collective agreements have transferred several ownership rights into the bargaining arena although the so-called residual rights are still exercised by management on behalf of the owners.

Gunnor Adler-Karlsson in *Reclaiming the Canadian Economy*: *A Swedish Approach through Functional Socialism* (Anansi 1970), describes how the Swedish Social Democratic government has shifted many other ownership rights from corporate managers to government policy-makers. These include some key decisions related to pricing and capital investments which are crucial to economic planning. Mr. Adler-Karlsson advocates an extension of functional socialism on the grounds that it works economically, it prohibits a concentration of power in any one group or class, and it gives the advantages of nationalization without the cost of compensating corporate owners.

Functional socialism appeals to social democrats and is expedient for Liberals and Conservatives. No Canadian government can resist the public pressure to reduce some of the worst abuses of corporate power. Liberals and Conservatives must balance their need for election funds from the corporations and the values they hold in common with those who control corporations, with their need for voters' support. Despite their inclinations, they are forced to grudgingly move towards functional socialism by limiting ownership rights and increasing public rights. At our current rate of movement, most of us will be long dead before we reach the point that Sweden has already reached. Nevertheless, we are going in that direction.

But how far can we go in that direction, and when we have gone as far as we can, what will we have accomplished?

We can open more 'residual' rights to collective bargaining. We can legislate more humane working conditions and minimum wages so reasonable working conditions will be assured even where unions are weak. We can require justification for price increases or make the market more competitive by expanding co-ops and public enterprises. We can control the direction of private investment to conform to an economic plan. We can legislate more consumer protection. And so on.

All of these are steps towards functional socialism in a mixed economy and all will develop a more equitable society — not as Adler Karlsson suggests, by spreading power throughout society, but as Galbraith suggests in his New Industrial State, by developing countervailing powers. But let us consider the next step — transfer of the right to make decisions to the people affected by those decisions. That is the essence of industrial democracy and it so completely eliminates the traditional rights of corporate ownership that the concept of ownership becomes meaningless.

This does not imply that public or government ownership must replace private ownership of enterprises but rather that we must start with a different concept.

The gut feeling of ownership is something we learn and is not a natural or inevitable state of man. Anthropological studies indicate that there are, and have been, many tribal groups with no concept of ownership even though there is respect for privacy and personal belongings. During my boyhood days in Northern Ontario, trapline cabins were never locked and it was recognized that the cabins and contents could be used by anyone in need. Respect was assumed but ownership was not a consideration.

The concept of ownership develops with shortages. When game and land are limited, the strong may lay exclusive claims. As society becomes more formalized, the exclusive claims are entrenched in law and the interaction of law, politics, property and theology works to create the gut feeling of private ownership and formal education reinforces it. With all of this, many young people are consciously rejecting the concept of ownership and many older people never acquired it. Cooperatives usually are supported by people with little gut feeling of ownership and this may explain their relative unpopularity in Ontario.

Wholesale nationalization of the means of production and distribution replaces one form of ownership with another. Whether the new form is better or worse depends upon who is in control and I am no more prepared to put such power of control in the hands of a few politicians and bureaucrats than I am to leave it in the hands of the corporate bosses. Nor am I prepared to be content with a system which depends on delicately balanced countervailing powers where one of those powers is derived from corporate ownership.

Let us take another look at corporate ownership. A corporation (traditionally known as a limited liability company) is a legal entity separate from its shareholders who are its owners. It comes into existence because one or more people have made application to the federal government or to a provincial government, requesting a charter (letters patent) for a company to be incorporated for specified purposes. Those purposes may be very restricted or very broad but are largely at the discretion of the people seeking the charter. Whether application is made to a provincial government or the federal government, depends mainly on whether or not business is going to be conducted in more than one province although certain kinds of businesses such as banking and insurance can only be incorporated federally.

When the charter has been granted, the corporation exists in law, although it consists only of a name and has no money. It gets its starting money (anything from a few dollars on up) by issuing shares in return for cash or other assets. Although the people who hold the shares are the corporation's owners, the corporation may obtain most of the money it needs to start operations from loans or government grants.

The recognition of corporations as legal entities is an artificial but convenient legal fiction which enables a corporation to conduct business, enter into contracts, sue and be sued and in other ways act as though it were a person without directly involving the owners. Because a corporation is a thing, and not a person, someone must sign contracts on its behalf, but contracts are signed on behalf of the corporation and not on behalf of its owners. In the event of corporate bankruptcy, the owners may lose any money invested in the corporation but they are not responsible for the corporation's debts.

Corporations and corporation owners are not only separate in law and in practice but, as Galbraith and others have demonstrated, corporate power is exercised by managers more than by owners although they have the same values. What, then, does it mean when we say that someone owns part or all of a corporation?

The simple answer is that the person owns some or all of the shares (capital stock) of the corporation. Proof of ownership is demonstrated by share certificates — fine looking pieces of paper attesting to ownership. To say that corporate ownership means ownership of pieces of paper attesting to ownership, tells us nothing. What do those pieces of paper attest to? What is the reality of a corporation?

A corporation may be made up of many assets such as cash, amounts owing from customers, inventories, furniture, machinery, buildings and land. It may have liabilities such as bank loans, debts to suppliers and bonds payable. The figure arrived at by subtracting measurable liabilities from measurable assets, gives something called shareholders' equity. That figure, presumably, is what the shareholders own although the most valuable thing in many corporations is the collective know-how of the employees and it is not one of the measurable, or measured, assets.

It may seem ridiculous to say that a shareholder owns part of the difference between two numbers, for that difference relates only to an abstract accounting and legal concept and has nothing to do with owning anything concrete, except that piece of paper attesting to ownership of an abstract concept. That piece of paper does not entitle its owner to go to the corporation and claim his interest in the corporate assets in return for paying off his interest in the corporate liabilities. He can recover his investment only by finding another buyer of his piece of paper. Suppose that other buyer was the corporation itself and suppose the corporation gradually bought back all of its shares, (and that is possible although presently subject to some legal restrictions) then the corporation would own itself. But as the corporation is just an artificial and convenient legal concept, how can it own itself?

This apparent paradox arises from a misuse of the word 'own', or at least the use of it in two very different senses. To return to an earlier reference, we cannot own a corporation as we own a toothbrush. If we want to use 'own' in relation to our toothbrush, we cannot use it in relation to corporations without confusion. It is much more reasonable to talk about investment in or control of, rather than ownership of, corporations.

Who, then, are the investors in corporations in the so-called private sector of our economy?

First, there are the people, or other corporations, who invest enough money to control the shares and thereby, the management in a new corporation. Second, there is usually the federal or a provincial or a municipal government or a combination of all three, which invests money or grants tax concessions to cover risks and to provide funds to acquire land, buildings and equipment. Next are the employees who invest their time, skills, brainpower, muscle power and, all too often, their lives. Then there is society as a whole which invests in the economic and educational infrastructure that enables the corporation to operate. Finally, there are the consumers who invest money in the products sold by the corporation, and if all goes according to plan, they will invest enough to refund, with interest, the original investment by shareholders. That is accomplished by the corporation paying dividends to the shareholders.

If everyone who invests in a corporation has an interest in it, and if everyone who has an interest in it should have a voice in its operation, we have an intriguing problem of determining in which spheres which voices should be dominant. There appear to be five main groups involved: the original investors in shares, the three levels of governments, society as a whole, consumers of the corporation's product and the employees. At present, the dominant voice is that of the investors in shares even though their investment is minimal in relation to total investment and is often recovered in a relatively short time. There is no need to perpetuate this. Its only justification was that private investment in shares was the main source of risk capital. It is no longer so.

If we wish to continue to provide opportunities for private investment, this can be done by allowing investment in bonds, debentures and similar types of loans protected by the usual laws covering financial obligations but not carrying any special powers. There is no need for private investment in equity because, as we have seen, the concept of owning equity is ridiculous and no longer relevant. In the major Japanese corporations, loans are the main source of capital and equity capital is insignificant.

Elimination of equity capital, and with it the concept of corporate ownership, need not adversely affect economic growth. In fact, it makes is easier to establish a more rational program for economic growth. It also allows us to concentrate on balancing the interests of the true investors — governments, society as a whole, employees and consumers. We need not worry about the elimination of equity capital adversely affecting the stock markets. Stock exchanges do not provide corporate capital, they are places where people bet on the fate of capital that has already been provided.

When stock brokers are no longer required to handle bets on the fate of capital, their talents can be used to handle bets on hockey, horses or the weather. The economic effect will be the same.

I cannot turn to Adam Smith, Karl Marx, or any reputable economist along the continuum between them, for my suggestion to eliminate shares or equity capital. The case for it has, however, been made many times by the Canadian Manufacturers Association, the Chamber of Commerce, numerous trade associations and many businessmen. They lobby with a consistent and constant theme: private capital will invest in shares of new corporations only if governments assume the risks. Their success in lobbying has taken away the only economic reasons for relating private investment to corporate ownership and control. It needs only a relatively simple change in legislation to bring the law into agreement with reality.

The change would eliminate shares (and thereby ownership rights) by converting them into bonds (debts) payable by the corporation to the former shareholders. Business itself has provided the precedent for this by creating so many different kinds of shares that many of them are almost indistinguishable from bonds. They have also created pieces of paper that can be converted from shares to bonds, or bonds to shares. A socialist government need only carry what capitalists are saying and doing, to its logical conclusion.

The problem of compensating shareholders when corporations are nationalized, does not arise if we convert equity capital to loan capital. Investors will be repaid as corporate profits permit so that both the value of their investments and the risk attached to it, remain unchanged. Their only loss is that gut feeling of ownership and related power. As compensation for that loss, there is their new opportunity to develop as people unfettered by alienating and antagonistic concepts of ownership and power.

You may now have seen the possibilities of using this device as a simple way of eliminating foreign ownership and transferring corporation control to Canada. And you may have dismissed it upon remembering the role of the U.S. Marines. If so, let me explain that I am not suggesting that the act can be accomplished in one stroke of the pen.

Throughout this book I have attempted to discuss what can be done now as steps towards the ideals outlined in the introduction. A sudden and complete elimination of the concept of corporate ownership would be a nice ego trip for socialists but it would do nothing to establish industrial democracy in a socialist society. It would, in fact, create a power vacuum which would be filled by bureaucrats not subject to the controls necessary to assure a transition to industrial democracy.

The experiment must be conducted selectively with the criteria for selection being simplicity, potential for dramatic results and availability of people to offer guidance during the transition.

Crown corporations already operating, rank first in terms of simplicity, and the initial steps towards industrial democracy can be taken immediately. In terms of potential results, mines are high on the list because so much can be done to improve working conditions and productivity. Political education can increase the supply of people to offer guidance.

Summary

Ownership is a vague word with several different meanings or implications. Ownership of corporations is not ownership in the usual sense. It is a legal concept which confers certain rights of control. The concept is unnecessary and because it is antagonistic and alienating, it should be eliminated. Nationalization just replaces one form of ownership with another. By completely eliminating the concept of corporate ownership, we can shift to the question of control and open the way to industrial democracy.

chapter twenty

reconciliation

IN the previous chapter, I suggested that people who have an interest in a corporation should have a voice in its operation. I also suggested that those who have an interest (after eliminating equity capital) include municipal, provincial and federal governments, society as a whole, consumers and employees. The problem is to reconcile the interest of employees managing their own work, with the other interest.

I have distinguished between governments and society as a whole in order to distinguish between parliamentary and extra-parliamentary activities. Governments act through formal channels and society as a whole acts and expresses its views through a variety of formal and informal organizations. Consumers are, of course, members of society, but are treated as a separate group because they have special interests as consumers.

It is impossible and unnecessary to establish relationships that function without disagreements. Disagreements and open debates are essential to freedom and progress providing the participants have common objectives. When the social and economic system is such that objectives of different groups or classes must conflict, then debate is not a part of the process of progress but a part of the struggle for power amongst competing groups. It is a struggle for a bigger slice of the pie and not for a better pie more equitably sliced.

Let us examine the relationships and areas of conflict in more detail.

A decision may be right when judged against the objectives of an enterprise, but wrong when judged against social objectives or desires. At present, our social objectives are partly determined by our desires for material needs and material luxuries which enhance our lives by providing convenience, comfort, amusement or beauty. Some of these desires are created artificially by our market economy. We want these things to be available with a combination of the lowest possible cost and highest possible quality. Decisions that aid in achieving these objectives are considered socially right.

In privately-owned corporations, the right decisions are those which maximize profits within certain legal constraints. More often than not, right decisions in the corporate context are wrong decisions in the social context. This conflict is well documented by E. J. Mishan in *Technology and Growth: The Price We Pay,* (Praeger 1969) where he discusses some of the adverse environmental and social effects of industrial expansion. On a more mundane level, we see examples of the conflict in:

(1) Model changes that add to cost but do not add to quality.
(2) Non-informative advertising that contributes nothing to our product knowledge but adds to the price.
(3) Corporations that leave quality control to customers who have the inconvenience of returning a new article for repairs.
(4) Corporations that exploit structural defects in the economy and oppose correction of the defects.
(5) Promotion of private rather than public transportation.

The list of conflicts between corporate and social interests, that is, between private benefit and public cost, could go on endlessly and attempts are made to reconcile them with the explanation that they contribute to the social objective of more employment. This is a valid point only if we think of high unemployment as the natural state of things, requiring relief by corporate action. It is not valid if we think in terms of mobilizing our resources to meet our social objectives. With that approach, the problem is not unemployment, but a shortage of labour and any waste slows down our progress towards those objectives.

This is all well known to socialists, but what is less well known, or perhaps, less often acknowledged, is that the advent of a socialist government does not automatically eliminate the conflicts between corporate and social objectives. This is so even if the corporations are publicly owned and profit is not the criterion of success. It is possible that if the election of a socialist government were immediately followed by the disappearance of all selfish interests and their replacement by full understanding of the effects of personal and corporate actions, no conflicts would exist. That, unfortunately, is unlikely to happen.

The elimination of equity capital, (corporation shares) as advocated in the previous chapter, eliminates one source of power conflicts. Elimination of authoritarian management eliminates another source of power conflicts. Nevertheless, these do not assure that workers in an industrial democracy setting will not engage in power struggles against social objectives.

Economic progress, which can be considered as one of our social objectives, depends upon effective use of our human and material resources. This, in turn, requires a mobile and adaptable labour force in order to cope with changing demands and new technology. But, in our work, most of us tend to be conservative and resist change when the effects of the change are uncertain or might adversely affect us.

Fear of unemployment is an important cause of our resistance to change. As we constantly have hundreds of thousands of people unemployed and many more under-employed, it is natural and right for unions and individuals to resist changes which lead to more unemployment. No pious statements about productivity, national interest or progress are going to make up for the difference between being employed or being unemployed. In no system are employees going to give their best when giving their best can lead to unemployment for themselves or their mates.

For humanitarian reasons, socialists are dedicated to eliminating unemployment. The elimination of the fear of unemployment is a prerequisite to effective industrial democracy but this requires more than maintaining what is usually described as full employment.

Full employment does not imply that everyone who wishes to work will always be able to work. Unless an economy were completely stabilized to the point of stagnation, there would always be people 'between jobs'. But there are differences between being unemployed and being between jobs. The differences are in the attitudes of the people not presently employed and in the attitudes of society towards them. For example, students attending colleges and universities are not employed but they do not feel unemployed, with the accompanying loss of dignity and feeling of being degraded, second-rate or unwanted. Society's attitude towards them, as reflected by governmental financial assistance, is that the students are engaged in a socially desirable activity.

Both the subjective and objective conditions of students are very different from those of men and women who make their daily rounds in search of work, their weekly trip to the Unemployment Insurance Office and finally the trip to the welfare office. That is a condition to be feared — not because of a danger of starvation, as it would hurt our 'image' if we allowed people to starve in Canada — but because of the degradation. To end that, a new approach to retraining, educational upgrading and relocation is required.

It is generally accepted that job training and retraining are important to economic growth and to specific enterprises in order to meet changing conditions. We attempt to anticipate change and arrange for retraining in time to meet it. Our success is limited first because of our inability to anticipate the direction of change and second, even when we guess right, we have to impose the idea of retraining. The person being retrained is the object of a plan originating elsewhere and the retraining may not be relevant to his work.

In a non-authoritarian organization controlled by the employees, direct experience would demonstrate the need for retraining — e.g. demand for product modifications or new service or loss in demand for current products or services. If the direct experience triggered the retraining, the motivation to retrain should be greater than if it is triggered externally and the nature of the retraining should be more in line with real needs.

The problem of time lag (delay between need for and accomplishment of retraining) should be less serious than at present because many employees now find it more reasonable to try to preserve redundant jobs rather than retrain for new ones. Most jobs now are means for livelihood, not a way of living. If, through industrial democracy, work can become part of living, then retraining can become a satisfying part of work instead of just a way to combat the threat of unemployment.

A change in attitude is necessary to accomplish this. We now have a fairly comprehensive retraining program, financed largely by the federal government, but it has a 'deserving poor' philosophy. To receive full retraining allowances, one must be categorized as unemployed and unemployable, then docilely accept the treatment accorded that category. It is analogous to the before-meal prayers at the Salvation Army, although I doubt if Salvation Army patrons are ever treated as contemptuously as Manpower Retraining patrons.

To be effective, retraining and upgrading programs must be an integral part of our attitude to work. Members of the professions are paid to attend conferences, seminars and work-shops to keep abreast of their fields. Professors are given leave with pay to study. Senior civil servants are paid to attend courses which might help them do their jobs. All this is accepted as an integral part of their work and no-one would suggest that doctors, lawyers, professors and civil servants should be forced to separate learning from working. Why then, can we not take the same attitude towards clerks, secretaries, factory workers, miners and lumberjacks.

It is economically sound. The direct cost of our massive unemployment and underemployment is far greater than an integrated work and training program with full employment, even if we ignore the indirect social costs of unemployment. And for industrial democracy to function effectively, continuing education, training and retraining essential to full employment, must be integrated in our attitude towards work and in the reality of working life. When this is done, workers can be free of the fear of unemployment which would otherwise prevent them from making decisions that would increase productivity in the interest of society as a whole.

According to capitalist mythology, unfettered free enterprise provides the best possible deal for consumers. The mythology persists even though every democratic government in industrialized countries has had to choose between restricting corporate exploition of consumers, or be voted out of office by consumers. Although we now have extensive legislation to protect Canadian consumers from some of the worst kinds of exploitation, most people would agree that the legislation is inadequate. It is inadequate because corporations and consumers have conflicting objectives and the legislation assumes common objectives. Even the most innocuous proposals for pro-consumer legislation run into heavy corporate opposition. This is a good indication that corporate managers recognize the conflict even if many consumers do not.

If the conflict is to be converted from a power struggle to a struggle towards common objectives, the causes of the conflict must be understood. They are the three main measures of corporate success: profit, growth, and share of the market.

Earlier in this chapter, I listed a number of actions that are right when profit is the criterion but wrong when consumers' interests are the criteria. The list could be expanded to include most decisions made to maximize profit.

Growth, in the form of an annual increase in the volume of business, influences management decisions as much as and possibly more than profit. Growth is, a priori, 'a good thing'. The management question is not 'Should we expand?' but 'How should we expand?' A manager might suggest a temporary entrenchment to improve the prospects for later expansion but if he were to suggest that the business was successful, and there was no need for more growth, his fellow managers would think he was some kind of nut. As they see growth as a measure of success, the suggestion would be meaningless.

The fastest way to grow is to get into new products or new lines of business and the fastest way to do that is by taking over other companies. The pursuit of fast growth is part of the reason for the conglomerate boom in the 1960's. So long as the conglomerates continued to acquire other companies, they were growing and therefore successful. In the process, they developed monstrosities that were impossible to manage, destroyed many smaller companies that had been at least partially responsive to their customers' wishes and made no positive contribution to the economy or the consumers.

Managers' dedication to growth is almost matched by their dedication to capturing a larger share of the market. To be successful, it is not enough to show annual growth. Managers must show that their products are gaining a larger share of the total market. If they sell $10 million of widgets this year and that represented twenty per cent of the total sales of widgets by all companies, next year they must aim for an increase in their share of the market from twenty to twenty-one per cent or more. That's success.

Dedication to a larger share of the market is strongest in industries producing goods that have a relatively fixed demand such as soap and food. We don't want a second bath when we have just had a bath, or a second meal when we have just eaten one, so the total potential sales of food and soap are limited. Each company therefore strives for a larger share of a limited market by using massive advertising campaigns and gimmicks. The fixed demand prevents increasing economies of scale from absorbing the cost of advertising and sales promotion, so the cost is borne by consumers.

These measures of success are deeply ingrained in most of us even though we may not articulate them in business terms. They influence us in non-commercial ventures including the operation of many universities, which have no equity capital or ownership rights, no profit motives and some involvement by workers in management. Although they cannot use profit as a measure of success, they can, and often do, measure success in terms of growth rate and share of the student market. The results are much the same as in commercial enterprises — universities become unmanageable conglomerates offering consumers a second-rate product.

If these same measures of success are applied to worker controlled industries in a socialist society, they will cause the same kind of conflict between workers and consumers as exists between corporations and consumers. And there is a danger that they will be applied and justified on the grounds that we must grow to achieve economies of scale. The weakness of that kind of justification is discussed elsewhere in this book.

There is no simple way to eliminate all conflicts between the interests of people as workers and as consumers although public awareness of some of the causes of conflict outlined above will help. I have considered various forms of consumer representation in enterprises but have rejected all of them, at least during the transition towards industrial democracy. Consumer representation might be desirable but it is not essential and would add a complicating factor in a delicate process. I believe that it is better to concentrate on industrial democracy and rely on education to bring the interests of consumers and workers closer. My feelings towards community or general public representatives in enterprises is much the same.

Using the currently popular 'systems approach' it is possible to develop a model which allows all interested groups to be represented in some appropriate enterprise body. The systems approach however requires such gross over-simplification that the resulting model would be misleading.

When we turn to the interests of federal, provincial and municipal governments, we must reconcile political democracy with industrial democracy. This is not as difficult as reconciling political democracy with industrial autocracy because there will be no inherent conflicts such as now exist between corporate and human interests. The conflicts will be more in the nature of disputes about the application of municipal, provincial and federal laws and regulations governing the location, operation and objectives of the enterprises. Work units fully integrated with self-governing communities (such as the Kibutzim in Israel, the communes in Yugoslavia and some Mennonite settlements in Canada) may develop from industrial democracy but we cannot now accept them as a means of reconciling worker and community interests.

Summary

For the process of industrial democracy to succeed, action at the political level will be necessary to eliminate antagonistic conflicts inherent in our present system. These include unemployment, private corporate ownership and the system of rewards that puts one segment of society against another. Our lack of ability to make these changes overnight should not be used as an excuse for not beginning the process of industrial democracy. On the contrary, the process itself will facilitate change.

chapter twenty-one

where to now?

WHEN I decided to write this book, I had no intention of writing about industrial democracy. My intention was to put forward proposals that would help make work more humane, more satisfying and more efficient. I wanted to expand some of the ideas contained in my articles on work techniques and organization, add others and find the common thread that would give them unity.

The common thread was elusive. I attempted to relate my work experience in Canada, the US and Sweden, to their economic and political systems, without much success. I thought that it would help to learn more about work organization in a country with a very different political and economic system.

Further research into relationships within enterprises led me slowly, and somewhat reluctantly, towards industrial democracy — reluctantly because its emotional appeal ran counter to all my business training and much of my business teaching. Most of the writing on industrial democracy has been done by Europeans or by people influenced by European writers. It tends to be considered inappropriate by most Canadians, including me. Nevertheless, I continued to gather evidence that demonstrated that fundamental change in work organization was possible and desirable. To accept the evidence I had to begin questioning practices I had accepted as right for many years.

I mention my personal reluctance to accept the concept of industrial democracy because I expect it will be shared by most of my readers and because it has influenced the style of much of this book. Often I have mentioned arguments against the ideas I have proposed. I was on the other side of those arguments not many years ago and I know the emotional and intellectual difficulties of rejecting conventions that we have accepted in the past. But assuming that we are now ready to break with convention, where do we go now?

It would be easier if we had a socialist government in Ottawa, but as I write, there is little prospect of that in the near future. There is some hope that an autonomous socialist party will develop in Quebec and cooperate with the N.D.P. at the federal level. If that happens, and if the Ontario N.D.P. stops trying to be all things to all people, then things may change in Ottawa. Meanwhile, the N.D.P. forms the government in only three provinces — Manitoba, Saskatchewan and British Columbia. Some of my recommendations go beyond the authority of provincial governments but that does not prevent the NDP governments from making a start on the road to industrial democracy. Nor does it preclude spontaneous action by workers.

Education, that most sacred of provincial rights, is important to the process of industrial democracy. As mentioned in my comments on Sweden, education cannot be politically neutral. Both its form and content reflect the values of those who have been in charge. Socialist governments must change the form to one in which pupils are encouraged to help one another, to participate in the educational process and to influence the school environment. The content must be changed so that pupils can become aware of the role of trade unions, cooperatives and other organizations that have pioneered in social reform. We must get away from the idea that individual heroes make history. Problems related to cooperatives and social benefits must be substituted for the mathematics problems requiring pupils to calculate profits on various commercial transactions. (Any reader who thinks I am stretching the point hasn't helped his children with mathematics homework.) The change in content will require a shift away from Canadian adaptations of American texts to home-grown texts.

The record of CCF and NDP provincial governments gives little cause for optimism. Although education is invariably the subject of lengthy debates in NDP provincial conventions, political power has not led to any fundamental changes in primary and secondary education.

True, a certain amount of tinkering has made schools more humane but they remain as institutions for training children to compete in a capitalist society. As this is being written, British Columbia offers the greatest hope for change but even there solutions are being sought without reference to a philosophic base.

There are a few obvious improvements that can be made, such as eliminating boards of governors controlled by businessmen, but the fundamental changes will come through applying the concepts of industrial democracy to universities. That cannot be done by continuing the endless debates about the ratio of students to teachers in university boards, senates and committees. Those debates presuppose a continuation of power struggles that must be resolved by representation in a hierarchical, authoritarian organization. Industrial democracy strives for direct participation and elimination of classifications that lead to power struggles. In universities those classifications include segregation of clerical, janitorial and maintenance staff so that they enjoy none of the privilege of belonging to an academic community.

Retraining and educational upgrading programs are financed largely by the Federal Government, but the provinces have some autonomy in administering the programs. Pressure will be required to obtain the flexibility needed to integrate those programs more closely with work life.

Related to retraining is the need for full employment which I have stressed in various chapters because unemployment and the fear of unemployment prevents workers from making decisions that could reduce job security. Some of the economic levers necessary to maintain full employment are controlled by the Federal Government. In particular, monetary policy is a federal matter, but provincial governments have political leverage that can make it difficult for the Federal Government to withhold cooperation in a plan for full employment even when that plan includes establishing socially-owned, self-managed enterprises. Although they have that leverage, it must be recognized that provincial governments can reduce but not eliminate unemployment unless there is a socialist government or a strong socialist threat in Ottawa. Recognizing that we cannot immediately end unemployment, we must recognize that some decisions made in democratically operated enterprises will be more influenced by a desire for job security than for efficiency. While this is not a desirable long term situation, in the short term it is both socially and economically more desirable than increased unemployment.

Throughout this book, I have touched on questions of American influence in our economy, trade unions, schools and universities. Obviously, that influence works against industrial democracy. But the converse is also true — industrial democracy works against and reduces that influence. Reduction in work alienation will lead to a reduction of the manifestations of alienation which symbolize the worst of American culture.

I don't wish to minimize the difficulties created by American influence. Nor do I wish to overstate them. Canada is not part of the USA. Our vertical mosaic may be similar but our ethnic and related cultural mosaic is very different. Our history and our present society is far less brutal than that of the US. We can choose from a wider range of political alternatives instead of being restricted to a choice between two capitalist parties. Most of all, we still have hope that it is not too late to reverse the tide of self-destruction.

What hinders us is a lack of self-confidence. A feeling that we are somehow second-rate. While we take a perverse pride in the fact that we can walk our streets at night in relative safety, we seem determined to repeat the mistakes made in the US. But it is not always so.

Much social legislation, such as universal government-sponsored hospital and medical care, was highly controversial when first introduced by the CCF in Saskatchewan. Although widely accepted now, it took courage and independence to introduce them at the time. In the 1940's, government hospitalization was as radical as industrial democracy in the 1970's.

It will take courage now to begin the process of industrial democracy. Courage based on the awareness that we can manage our own affairs within our country and within our enterprises.

Before writing this book, I considered myself to be a "democratic" manager. My staff participated in all policy matters and the decisions made usually reflected their views, although formal votes were not taken. When I was approached with an idea, I usually said something like, "Work it through, decide what you want to do, present it to me and if everything is okay I will approve it."

The hierarchies demanded my signature of approval on many things emanating from my staff, but it does not follow that I had to be the one to decide if "everything is okay". If the people working under my direction had all the relevant information, there was no reason for them to make recommendations for my approval. They would be as well or better able than I, to decide what should be done. When I realized that the veto power I retained was inconsistent with my beliefs and writings, I was determined to eliminate the inconsistency. Instead of, "If everything is okay I will approve it", I felt I must switch to, "These are the resources we have to work with and you know what you want to accomplish. Work out the details and if my signature of approval is required, I will give it."

The advanced commitment to approval was difficult at first because it meant giving up the security of final control. In its place was the knowledge that my staff would not make irresponsible decisions because they were given full responsibility, but still it wasn't easy to give up the Linus blanket. It was easy for me to rationalize that I had to control the things for which I accepted responsibility. To break away from this rationalization I had to recognize that the best decisions would be made by those directly involved in doing the job, providing they had the necessary background information. My job, therefore, was to provide that information to them, and not keep it to myself so as to retain control or power.

This "confession" is not given by way of apology. It is intended to illustrate the difficulties faced by managers in a transitional period. The same difficulties will be faced by those who make policy at the senior levels of governments. To break through requires an act of faith. It is my hope that this book would make the act of faith easier.

Industrial democracy is a process. It is a process which we can begin now and when successful it will go beyond anything we can now envisage. The process itself is liberating. Its failure would be marked by its termination. Its success will be demonstrated by its continuation.

So it was with political democracy. So it will be with industrial democracy.

Let us begin now.

references

PREREQUISITES

My prerequisites or basis for industrial democracy diverge from most writing on the subject. Most advocates of industrial democracy have different starting points. There are some who see industrial democracy, or more specifically, workers' control, as a tactic in a broader revolutionary struggle to transfer power to the proletariat.

Prominent amongst this group is the French writer, Andre Gorz. His book, *Strategy for Labour* has been published in English by Beacon Press (1967). More typical of North American advocates of industrial democracy are those who are influenced by a concern for community involvement. A number of Fellows at the Cambridge Institute in Massachusetts have done some serious papers from this point of view. They include John Case and Barry Stein, amongst others. In Canada, Black Rose Books has published a number of books and pamphlets which tend towards a community participation approach. They include *Participatory Democracy for Canada,* edited by Gerry Hunnius, and *The New Left in Canada* edited by Dimitrios I. Roussopoulos. A book by George

Benello and Dimitrios Roussopoulos, *The Case for Participatory Democracy,* is published by Grossman Publishers (New York) and distributed by Fitzhenry and Whiteside in Canada. Also available from Black Rose Books is a kit on workers' control which includes a fairly wide range of pamphlets.

Special mention must be made of work done by Gerry Hunnius of Praxis: Institute for Social Change in Toronto. Gerry Hunnius is the author or editor of numerous books, pamphlets and articles on industrial democracy. Any serious student of the subject is soon referred to Mr. Hunnius, and like many others I am grateful for his help.

My remarks on Canadian labour related largely to unions affiliated to the Canadian Labour Congress and may not be relevant to the situation in Quebec, which is somewhat more volatile than in the rest of Canada. In this connection, *Quebec Labour,* published in 1972 by Black Rose Books is useful.

For more information on the carry-over of work to non-work life, see *The Long Arm of the Job* by Martin Meissner, *(Industrial Relations: A Journal of Economy & Society,* Vol. 10, No. 3: October 1971), reprinted in *Canada: A Sociological Profile,* W. E. Mann, ed. (2nd edition, Toronto: Copp Clark, 1971)

POWER AND AUTHORITY

Many books on political science, history, sociology and anthropology discuss power and authority; however, within those disciplines the words are used in a different sense from my usage. The distinction I have made between power and authority is a subjective one and it is a valid distinction insofar as it helps us understand our reactions to different circumstances.

Readers wishing to take a closer look at those reactions will find the following books interesting:

Work, edited by Ronald Fraser, (Penguin 1968)

Work II, edited by Ronald Fraser, (Penguin 1969)

Each of these contains 20 personal accounts of work. They make no pretence of being anything other than that, but they effectively illustrate the similarity of the pressures on workers whether they are in coal mines, steel mills or stockbrokers' offices. *Work II* is the more representative collection.

Carr's *The Business Game,* (Signet 1969), is a collection of amoral advice for executives who want to acquire power in corporations. In some ways it complements the "Work" books mentioned above.

TRADE-OFFS

My comments about the unwillingness of mining companies to take risks may seem to be contradicted by the well known risk of investing in shares of mining companies. There is, however, almost no connection between mining and shares in mining companies. For readers who want more information on this topic, I would recommend *The Stock Promotion Business,* (McLelland & Stewart, 1967).

Government handouts to business were a major issue in the 1972 federal election campaign. For a documented account see *Louder Voices: The Corporate Welfare Bums* by David Lewis, (James & Samuel, 1972).

Remarks on conservative and socialist attitudes towards security are based partly on theories advanced by Charles Hampden-Turner in his book *Radical Man,* (Schenkan, 1970, Anchor Books, 1971). This book is an important contribution to our understanding of human behaviour and I strongly recommend it to anyone prepared to struggle through an unfamiliar labyrinth. This book has not attained the popularity it deserves, perhaps because it is difficult to read until you get used to the vocabulary and because it attacks some cherished academic myths.

Industrial Democracy: The Sociology of Participation by Paul Blumberg, (Constable, 1968), is mentioned in the text. I would recommend this book to serious students of industrial democracy and to readers who want a general overview of the subject.

I quoted from Erich Fromm's *The Revolution of Hope: Toward a Humanized Technology,* (Bantam, 1968). This book is not as well known as some other books by Dr. Fromm, but it does deal with some aspects of industrial democracy. No recommendation is necessary for readers already familiar with Dr. Fromm's writings. For others, I could not give a strong enough recommendation. See also *The Art of Loving,* (Bantam, 1963) and *Marx's Concept of Man,* (Frederick Ungar Publishing Co. 1961), by Dr. Fromm.

ARE MANAGERS NECESSARY?

The management process summarized at the beginning of this chapter is expanded in all of several dozen introductory text books on management principles. For a more amusing approach to the subject, read *Management and Machiavelli* by Antony Jay, (Penguin, 1967). Jay illustrates some of the more ridiculous aspects of management in large corporations by analogy with the royal courts of the middle ages.

A more recent book by Antony Jay, *Corporation Man,* (Jonathon Cape Ltd.1972), attempts to compare primitive tribal behaviour with corporate behaviour. The topic would have made a good essay but was unfortunately stretched into a book. Worth reading if you get a free copy.

TECHNOLOGY AND ORGANIZATION

The following quotation is taken from *Technology Today* by Edward de Bono, (Routledge and Kegan Paul, London, 1971).

"One can live in the technological age as a zombie who does what he is told. Or one can live in the technological age as a zombie who objects to everything he is told. But if one wants to take part in the technological decisions and policy one needs to know something more about it than blanket refusal or blanket acceptance. And since technology has become man's biggest danger it is useful to be able to exert some control over it. To do this one does not need to know the complete details of every aspect of technology but something of the principles and processes and possibilities."

Technology Today demonstrates that we need not be dehumanized victims of modern technology but can in fact use our knowledge to help create a more humane society.

Master the Snapshot, an article by Hattersley in the January 1972 edition of *Popular Photography,* warns of the dangers of professional photographers becoming so wrapped up in their skills at handling complex equipment that they lose the instincts and insights of amateurs. The article has application well beyond the field of photography.

Computer Art and Human Response by Lloyd Sumner, (Paul B. Victorius, 1968), is a sensitive and beautifully illustrated book. Mr.

Sumner demonstrates how computers can be used as tools for artists just as paintbrushes can be used. His work and his life show that it is possible to integrate advanced technology with humanist philosophies.

QUANTITATIVE MANAGEMENT TECHNIQUES AND COMPUTERS

Unfortunately, I am unable to provide many references for laymen other than my own writings on these subjects. Books and articles on computers tend to be written for specialists or distorted for popular consumption. An exception to this is *Computers, Managers & Society* by Michael Rose, (Penguin, 1969). Quantitative management techniques is a subject which seems to be reserved exclusively for the specialists.

My articles on these topics include *Don't Let Your Computer Operations Fail,* first published in *Canadian Business* magazine in June 1971 and reprinted in *Canadian Business Concepts* edited by J. G. Sayers, (Holt, Rinehart & Winston, 1972). (This book provides an unconventional and interesting introduction to business.)

High Costs of Management Rough on People and Purses, Canadian Transport, April 1, 1972, by H. B. Wilson. In *Culture & Management,* (Irwin, ed. Ross E. Webber, 1969) is a chapter by Solomon John Rowan called *The Manager in the Polish Enterprise,* first published in the British Journal of Industrial Relations, March 1965. The material is out of date but it is a good analysis of how managers manipulate to show up well in the quantitative control systems. The writer seems to be unaware that the phenomenon which he observed in Poland applies equally to private enterprise in the western world.

COMMITTEES

Most readers will have served on so many committees they will have little desire to spend more time reading about them. I would, however, like to refer you to the following quotation from *Doing Business In Japan,* (Sophia University, ed. R. J. Ballon, p. 25, Ch. 1)

"In fact, all authority comes from responsibility; responsibility comes from the task which has been assigned; and the assignment of the task comes from the general law of harmony which regulates the whole."

MOTIVATION

There is no shortage of material on this subject, but I would like to single out a few sources. *The Neurotic Personality of Our Time* by Karen Horney, (Norton, 1937), provides a good account of the impact of conflicting values in a competitive system of society. *Management and the Social Sciences* by Tom Lipton, (Penguin Modern Management Texts, 1971), is a good illustration of how liberals draw on social sciences to manipulate employees without realizing what they are doing. An article in the July-August 1971 *Harvard Business Review* by Thomas H. Fitzgerald entitled *Why Motivation Theory Doesn't Work,* is of interest because Mr. Fitzgerald is an experienced executive in the automobile industry and he demonstrates the fallacy of conventional motivation theory.

For a satirical treatment of the subject, see *A Misguided Tour* by H. B. Wilson in the February 1, 1969, edition of *Canadian Transport,* reprinted in March 12, 1969, edition of *Commonwealth.*

PROFITS

The Elusive Art of Accounting by H. R. Ross, (Ronald Press, 1966) is one of the few books on accounting of interest to both specialists and laymen. Strongly recommended for anyone who wants to pursue this subject without trying to penetrate the mysteries of debits and credits.

Social Accounting: Measuring the Unmeasurables by Gerald H. B. Ross, an article in *Canadian Chartered Accountant* magazine, July 1971, suggests pushing out the boundaries of accounting to include some social considerations that are now excluded. Good introduction to the problem but offers few solutions.

In the Name of Profit by Robert L. Heilbroner and others, (Doubleday, 1972), makes fascinating, if somewhat horrifying reading. It is a collection of accounts of disreputable behaviour in several leading US corporations — including knowingly endangering lives to increase profits. People and companies are named and include General Motors, B.F. Goodrich and Merrill Drugs. The summation by Heilbroner suggests that such actions are typical of large corporations and are inevitable in a profit-oriented economy.

RULES AND REGULATIONS

The Railroad Switchman by John Spier, (Berkeley Journal of Sociology, Vol. 5, No. 1, Fall 1959), is an interesting account of ". . . the prototype of that half-disciplined proletarian, the railroad man . . ." It includes a description of rule-bending.

Also about railroads is a presently unpublished mimeographed manuscript by R. E. (Lefty) Morgan of North Vancouver. To explain the inclusion of this reference, I will quote from a letter I wrote to Mr. Morgan on October 24, 1972:

> "This past weekend I read your manuscript on railroad workers and I would like permission to make reference to it in my forthcoming book on industrial democracy. Specifically, I would like to refer to it as an unpublished manuscript which I hope will soon be published and which I strongly recommend to my readers because I believe it shows remarkable insights."

In a later discussion, Mr. Morgan indicated that he would seek a publisher for his ms.

BIGNESS

The election of an NDP government in B.C. in 1972 shows some reaction against the "big is good" mythology. The NDP had a no-growth policy emphasizing production quality instead of quantity.

My attack on the conventional theories of economies of scale is based largely on my own observations and substantiated by the fact that small companies in countries such as Sweden and Norway compete effectively against the international giants.

INTERNATIONAL

My comments on various European countries were deliberately restricted to points that I felt were of relevance to industrial democracy in Canada. I recognize, however, that some readers may want more detailed information. For those readers there is no shortage of material, but there is a problem sorting out the propaganda from the facts. As a good factual introduction to several countries I would recomment *Economic Consultative Bodies: Their Origins and Institutional Characteristics* by Paul Malles, (Economic Council of Canada, Information Canada, 1971).

Free Labour World published by ICFTU has carried numerous articles on industrial democracy throughout most of western Europe. Many of the 1971 editions of the magazine contain one or more such articles.

Much of the reference material I have used in the sections on Germany, Sweden and Norway was obtained in those countries and is not readily available in Canada, nor is it all available in English. It is possible, however, to obtain English copies of the highlight of *Labour Regulations* in each of these countries as well as copies of the master agreements between the employers' federations and the unions. The easiest way to obtain these is through the embassies.

Pamphlets and articles on Yugoslavia are so numerous and reflect such a range of opinions that I am reluctant to single out any one of them. For the serious student I would recommend an unpublished thesis written in September 1970 by Alan Whitehorn, available through Carleton University in Ottawa, with the title *Yugoslavia Workers' Councils — An experiment in industrial democracy*. This thesis gives a good factual account of the development of self-management in Yugoslavia and contains an extensive bibliography.

ECONOMICS

There are endless books on Economics and one sometimes gets the impression that many of them are written with the intention of confusing rather than enlightening. Readers seeking a straightforward introduction to the subject might try *Understanding Macro-economics* by Robert L. Heilbroner, (Prentice-Hall Inc. 1965). For a lucid analysis of the economic-political system in the U.S. J. K. Galbraith's *The New Industrial State*, (Houghton Mifflin hardcover, Mentor Pocketbook, 1968) is recommended. For an analysis of the effects of the Canadian economic system, see *The Real Poverty Report,* by Ian Adams et al, (M. G. Hurtig Limited, 1971).

CANADA
AND RADICAL
SOCIAL CHANGE

MORE BOOKS
FROM

BLACK
ROSE
BOOKS

edited by
Dimitrios
Roussopoulos

This collection of outstanding essays on various social questions in Canada are taken from the radical quarterly journal, OUR GENERATION which was founded in 1961. The journal, which has the highest circulation among the publications of this type in the country, has made a lasting contribution to the serious discussion concerning the Canadian social crisis.

The essays deal with unemployment, youth politics, poverty, economic continentalism, the new left, urban renewal, electoralism, and parliamentary democracy, and the student revolt.

Contributors include some of our most outstanding commentators: Fred Caloren, B. Roy Lemoine, Philip Resnick, Gerry Hunnius, George Grant, Jim Harding, Evelyn Dumas, Mel Watkins, Jim Laxer, Christian Bay, and many others. *250 pages / Hardcover $9.95 / Paperback $2.95*

Send for
complete catalogue
free

ISBN : 0-919618-10-3 / ISBN : 0-919618-09-x
BLACK ROSE BOOKS No. D12

156

LET THE NIGGERS BURN!

Racism in Canada

The Sir George Williams
Affair and its
Caribbean Aftermath

edited by

Dennis Forsythe

From the black point of view, Dennis Forsythe, who teaches sociology at Sir George Williams University has edited a collection of essays by other blacks which include: the problems of the black immigrant, the background to the "Anderson Affair" at Sir George Williams and what happened and the subsequent upheaval in the Caribbean area.

These and other essays in the book contribute to the publication of an important book in the growing literature of social criticism in Canada.

Contributors include: Delisle Worrell, Bertram Boldon, Leroi Butcher, Carl Lumumba, Roosevelt Williams, and Rawle R. Frederick.

200 pages / Hardcover $6.45 / Paperback $2.45
ISBN : 0-919618-16-2 / ISBN : 9-919618-17-0

BLACK ROSE BOOKS No. B4
Library of Congress Catalog Card Number : 73-76057

THE POLITICAL ECONOMY OF THE STATE

Canada / Québec / USA

edited by
Dimitrios Roussopoulos

This new book subjects the State in our society to a rigourous examination. Both the enormous growth of the State bureaucracy and the myth of its neutrality in social and economic affairs is carefully studied. Rick Deaton in *"The Fiscal Crisis of the State in Canada"*, deals with the whole range of activities in the public sector as well as the enormous growth of the Federal State, while B. Roy Lemoine in *"The Growth of the State in Québec"* examines the new role and function of the State since the "quiet revolution". Graeme Nicholson in *"Authority and the State"* studies the relationship of authoritarian patterns of behaviour and hierarchical institutions which are inter-laced with the State at their highest expression, while John and Margaret Rowntree in *"Revolution in the Metropolis"* submit a major essay that pulls many of the themes of the book together. Finally Lorne Huston comments on the effect of *Local Initiative Projects* and *Opportunities for Youth* grants on citizens groups.

The Political Economy of the State begins an important new approach to the study of government and society which political science has ignored for a very long time.

200 pages / Hardcover $9.95 / Paperback $2.95
ISBN : 0-919618-02 / ISBN : 0-919618-01-4

BLACK ROSE BOOKS No. D8

QUEBEC LABOUR STRIKES

by Arnold Bennett

Since the publication of the widely acclaimed "Québec Labour", the greatest General Strike in North American labour history has taken place. A Common Front of the Confederation of National Trade Unions, the Québec Federation of Labour, and the Québec Teachers Corporation while in a protracted struggle with the Québec government provoked a spontaneous revolt of some 350,000 workers in public service as well as private industry. What are the facts behind this upheaval? What has happened to the labour movement since the General Strike? What does the breakaway CSD trade union represent? What has happened to the growing radicalisation of the teachers union? How has all this affected the whole social movement consisting of the multitude of citizen committees, tenant associations, welfare recipients, unemployed workers, community medical and legal clinics and so on? These and many other related questions are examined in this thoroughly documented book.

225 pages / Hardcover $9.95 / Paperback $2.95
ISBN : 0-919618-1 / ISBN : 0-919618-07-3

BLACK ROSE BOOKS No. D11

THE GENOCIDE MACHINE
in Canada

The Pacification of the North

by Robert Davis
and Mark Zannis

In the preface, Montreal journalist Boyce Richardson writes, "Zannis and Davis are two amazing fellows. They never cease to gnaw away at the mighty tree of the financial and political establishment, like a couple of beavers; they are not only anxious to bring something crashing down, but also want to build." Further on Richardson writes, "There is no doubt in my mind that most Canadians will be surprised by what Zannis and Davis have found out about what is happening in the Canadian North . . ." "The case they make is extremely powerful."

This thoroughly documented book on the Canadian North and its people will shock the reader. It deals with various military projects, government departments, the courts, the RCMP, and their relations with the North. The question of the 'scientific' planning of various institutes like the Arctic Institute of North America is also examined in the light of the United Nations Convention on Genocide.

$3.95 paper / $10.95 hardcover